IDAHO POLITICS AND GOVERNMENT

Politics and Governments
of the American States

Founding Editor
DANIEL J. ELAZAR

Published by the University of Nebraska Press
in association with the Center for the Study of
Federalism at the Robert B. and Helen S. Meyner
Center for the Study of State and Local
Government, Lafayette College

Idaho
Politics and
Government

CULTURE CLASH AND CONFLICTING
VALUES IN THE GEM STATE

JASPER M. LICALZI

UNIVERSITY OF NEBRASKA PRESS

LINCOLN AND LONDON

Library of Congress Cataloging-in-Publication Data
Names: LiCalzi, Jasper M., author.
Title: Idaho politics and government:
culture clash and conflicting values in
the Gem State / Jasper M. LiCalzi.
Description: Lincoln: University of Nebraska Press,
2019. | Series: Politics and governments of the
American states | Includes bibliographical
references and index.
Identifiers: LCCN 2017056175
ISBN 9780803286894 (pbk.: alk. paper)
ISBN 9781496210609 (epub)
ISBN 9781496210616 (mobi)
ISBN 9781496210623 (pdf)
Subjects: LCSH: Idaho—Politics and
government. | Political culture—Idaho.
Classification: LCC JK7516 .L53 2019 |
DDC 320.4796—dc23
LC record available at
https://lccn.loc.gov/2017056175

Set in Minion Pro by E. Cuddy.

To Deborah,
love always

CONTENTS

Acknowledgments

My father always harried me about writing a book: that is what college professors do. I felt, until now, that I did not have enough to write about. More than twenty years of living and observing the political economy of Idaho has finally allowed me to have what I believe to be an important point to make about my adopted home. My one regret is my father is not here to read the book.

I want to thank the College of Idaho for providing me with an extended period of time to write. The library staff helped me immeasurably in obtaining the source material I needed much more quickly than I thought possible.

I want to thank the colleagues in my department, both past and present. When I first came to Idaho, Orv Cope, my former colleague, gave me a copy of Randy Stapilus's *Paradox Politics* and advised me to read it to learn about Idaho politics. That is where my study of the state really began. Jim Angresano, now retired from the college, always provided the perfect example to me of rigorous research and scholarship in the discipline. I want to especially thank my current colleagues Kerry Hunter and Rob Dayley for picking up the slack in the department during my sabbatical and for all of their assistance and guidance through the years.

I want to thank all of my students, without whom none of this would be possible. Your questions and constant desire to learn inspired me to push myself to be better in the classroom and as a researcher. I believe I learn more from my students than they learn from me.

I want to thank the people at University of Nebraska Press for all of their help with this publication. I would especially like to acknowledge Robert Taylor, who persevered from the beginning; Joeth Zucco, who pulled together the final product; Maureen Bemko, the freelancer who polished the manuscript with incredible copyediting, and Courtney Ochsner and Ann Baker, who provided assistance along the way.

The warmest and sincerest thanks go to the best academic assistant any faculty member has ever had: Lucinda Wong. With her mighty blue pencil, Lucinda's superior editing skills, relentless attention to details, and tireless efforts turned a sloppy mass of ideas and words into a book I am proud of. Any errors of style or substance are, of course, mine and mine alone.

This book, like everything in my life since I was twenty years old, is only possible due to my loving wife, Deborah. All I am and all I ever accomplish I owe to her.

Introduction

On February 27, 2012, Chuck Winder, state senator from Meridian, introduced legislation that would become known informally as the ultrasound bill. Styled after a bill introduced though not passed in the Virginia state legislature, Winder's bill, according to its language, sought to strengthen the ability of women to have "informed consent" before undergoing an abortion. Under the law an ultrasound would have to be performed and the patient would be given the opportunity—stated as a "right" in the legislation—to view the ultrasound, hear the heartbeat, and receive a picture from the ultrasound. In addition to provisions in the bill assuring the availability of printed materials (e.g., about adoption services), a description of the fetus, a description of the abortion procedure, and a list of facilities where one could get a free ultrasound, providing a woman with the results of the mandatory ultrasound was seen as an integral part of a woman's informed consent.[1]

Heightened interest in the bill began when the implications of the ultrasound for women in the early stages of their pregnancies were revealed. Although a traditional abdominal ultrasound would be sufficient in some cases to provide a clear picture of the fetus, "an invasive transvaginal ultrasound, a procedure that includes penetration of the patient with an ultrasound wand," would be necessary in cases of early-stage pregnancy.[2] Proponents of the legislation tried to downplay the disturbing nature of the procedure by having demonstrations of it under controlled conditions in the state capitol. Regardless, opponents of the legislation echoed the feelings of a female legislator in Virginia who described the procedure as "state-mandated rape."[3]

Initially the ultrasound legislation sailed through the Idaho state legislature. The senate's State Affairs Committee passed the bill along party lines, 7–2. The State Affairs Committee in the senate acts as an arm of leadership and is dominated by both party leaders and legislators loyal to leadership. Many controversial or incendiary bills in the senate are routed to State Affairs. Since the sponsor of the bill, Chuck Winder, was the assistant majority leader in the senate and a member of the committee, it was logical for the ultrasound bill to go to this committee.[4]

On the senate floor the first chinks in the armor of Winder's ultrasound bill were exposed. Prominent Republican legislators began to question both the substance and the political purpose of the bill. Shawn Keogh of Sandpoint noted the bill had been advocated by her primary challenger. Keogh provided the first argument that showed this issue did not cleave simply on party lines or traditional issue positions. Touting her "pro-life" credentials, Senator Keogh felt uncomfortable with the State of Idaho mandating medical procedures. She raised the question of how this legislation would fit in with the role of government: "What place do we as a government have in that room with that patient and with that doctor?"[5]

The final vote on the floor of the Idaho senate showed that some "conservative" Republican legislators were more concerned with the liberties of the individual (i.e., the woman seeking an abortion) than with the concerns of the community (i.e., the welfare of the unborn). Although the vote was still a lopsided 23–12, five Republicans, principally from traditionally libertarian North Idaho, joined all the Democrats in the chamber in opposing the bill. The bill would move on to the house chamber, but now that it was apparent that reactions to the bill did not split strictly on partisan lines, easy passage was not guaranteed.[6]

The ultrasound bill was assigned to the house's own State Affairs Committee, but no hearings were scheduled. Without scheduling hearings on the bill, the chair of the committee, again through the guidance of Republican Party leaders in the house, effectively killed the bill. Although no house Republicans would go on record concerning the proceedings of the closed party caucus, it is assumed that Republicans in the Idaho house chose not to deal with this issue. Darrell Bolz, a Republican from libertarian-leaning Canyon County, did note, "It's mixed emotions with me, but I have some real concerns about it." Echoing the dichotomy of values expressed by Senator Keogh, Bolz continued, "We talk about government invasiveness into people's lives. . . . I'm pretty much for right-to-life, but I have to represent my constituents."[7]

A bill supported by national groups opposed to abortion seemed at least initially to be a natural for conservative "red-state" Idaho. These outside groups, not aware of the dynamics of the state, tried to fit the defeat of the bill into the national dialogue of liberal versus conservative. Some commentators unfamiliar with Idaho saw the defeat of the bill to be the work of "abortion backers." This view was especially prominent in the postmortem performed by the Cornerstone Family Council.[8] No one with any familiarity with Senator Keogh or Representative Bolz would have called either of them an "abortion backer." The problem with this analysis of the bill's demise is the focus on abortion. The ultrasound bill morphed from an abortion bill to a bill that pitted libertarian values against the communitarian values of the people of Idaho.

Dan Popkey, a prominent Idaho political observer and journalist, saw the conflict within the state personified by the governor's position. Noting in an op-ed article Gov. C. L. "Butch" Otter's previous stances against mandatory immunization, a "health conscience" bill, and coercion by the federal government to raise the state drinking age, Popkey framed the debate over ultrasounds as a contest between Otter's Catholic faith and libertarian "secular principle." Popkey's subheading for his article ("Idaho's champion of individual liberty is likely to face a choice between competing values") succinctly characterizes the governor's internal quandary over the rights of the individual versus society as a whole.[9] This struggle over requiring ultrasounds before abortions exemplifies the conflicting values that are in constant tension in the state and even within individuals.

CULTURE CLASH

Politics has been seen as the socialization of conflict. How does society ameliorate the inevitable differences in preferences among its members? How can people settle disputes concerning fundamental human values? Most basically, How can everyone just get along? The manner in which society answers these questions is based on the divisions present in society and, as noted above, within members of society. One must understand what separates individuals before it becomes possible to discover mechanisms, institutions, conventions, or dictates that would provide a means for obtaining an acceptable balance between the differing values people hold.

It has become customary to see the divides in American society along simple fractures of broad ideology (liberal versus conservative), political party (Democrat versus Republican), or some combination of the two. This typology can be helpful in understanding certain situations and is basic enough for people to understand without an in-depth understanding of a situation or environment. These categorizations of conflicting values tend to fall apart when viewed on a subnational level and even more so as one reaches the level of the individual citizen. When the social scientist or political observer labels states, regions, and even persons as liberal or conservative, one simplifies the complex to a degree that accuracy is sacrificed for nominal minimalism. Painting society with only two colors of beliefs is not inherently disingenuous if one understands and appreciates the various hues that are created by the mixing of colors into secondary tints that may more accurately describe the landscape of society. The example of the ultrasound bill in Idaho shows that trying to explain the complex divisions in society through current diagnostic tools yields a vague picture.

Probably the most widely acclaimed and cited typology of American ideology on the subnational level is Daniel Elazar's work on political subcultures. Any study of state and local politics would be remiss without at least a footnote paying homage to Elazar and his pathbreaking work. The concept that Americans can be rounded up into only a few corrals of complementary yet conflicting visions of the role of government in society and the role of the citizen in society is both intoxicating and palliative. Settlement and migratory patterns can offer a means of categorizing the states, placing each into one of the primary subcultures or a hybrid mixture, with one category dominant over another.[10] When studying a state as complex as Idaho, one might benefit by looking first at subcultures.

Some observers of states, including observers of Idaho, have tried to isolate different subcultures into regions within the state. Although such studies are an interesting and at times stimulating endeavor, these efforts attempt to show the strength of a subculture in a region at the expense of looking for the underlying conflict among and within individuals—a conflict that shapes the political process and the substantive results of that process. Asking individuals questions about beliefs and substantive issues in order to classify regions into categories of subculture provides limited assistance in attempting to understand the forces that influence the lives of individuals through the collective action of society.

Studying the institutions, both governmental and quasi-governmental, of a state through the lens of conflicting visions of what government should do and how members of society experience their political world is a meaningful approach to the study of the political nature of society. Although similar projects have been undertaken in other states, including Colorado, Oregon, Arizona, and Kansas, no comprehensive study of both the political history and institutions of Idaho has been completed using subcultures as an assessment tool.

WHAT THIS BOOK IS AND WHAT IT IS NOT

Often it is clearer to conceive of an object when one knows what it is not. Many books try to accomplish too much or seek to achieve a goal that is beyond the stated focus. There is much that this book is not. What it *is* should come into focus when its parameters are identified in detail.

This book is not a dissertation on ideology and political culture. There is a chapter that provides limited background on previous works on political subcultures and their relationship with state politics, but that serves only as a backdrop to a framework showing how individuals attempt to understand the social phenomenon they experience. A modified version of the topology used by others is applied to the institutions, events, and individuals of Idaho.

Instead of subculture, which arises from migratory patterns and implies a grounding that is much deeper than politics, a derivative is developed that focuses more on political ideology in a circumscribed manner. Limiting ideology to a narrow spectrum of subjects and beliefs, the ensuing formula allows analysis of various individuals and political phenomena in order to explain what some have seen as the paradox of Idaho politics.[11] I have chosen to call this new typology "petit-ideology." This measure of one's beliefs is not as "large" as ideology is traditionally thought, since one's ideology encompasses broad swaths of a person's understanding of the world, especially concerning ideas and ideals of political economy.

My measure is "smaller," hence the term "petit," which I borrowed from the French due to the word's concise manner of conveying the concept of being minor or secondary. Petit-ideology focuses on the tension between liberty for individuals and the public good or benefits that would accrue to the community as a whole. These two ideological poles have their origins in the opposing views of founding fathers Thomas Jefferson and Alexander Hamilton, and their names are convenient, easily remembered labels for the two dominant types of political belief in the United States. This book offers an examination of prominent individuals and issues in Idaho history and of the effort to find a pragmatic middle ground as a means of governing amid the tension inherent in petit-ideology.

While using petit-ideology to aid in our understanding of political phenomena in Idaho, this book does not attempt to explain every person, occurrence, and institution through a single variable. There is no claim to a universal explanation for human behavior and thought. The use of petit-ideology is a means and method to see the world, or at least a small corner of the world in Idaho, in a different, nonstandard manner. There is no assertion that this process is unique, exclusive, or even optimal.

This book is also not a test of the applicability of petit-ideology. This is a theory-building exercise. Before extensive empirical studies are performed, a well-constructed case study can help ensure that the variables to be tested are properly identified. A study of a particular situation can increase our knowledge of the relevant variables in an action situation. It can also provide us with greater knowledge of the significance of the causal relationships to be tested. A case study can be employed in this instance as a heuristic device. It can be used to stimulate interest and further investigation. A properly configured case study can focus attention on special variables and significant relationships.[12] Petit-ideology is a new means by which one can understand the political context of society and the individual.

This book does not provide a comprehensive political history of the state of Idaho. It thus does not include a history of the state from its "discovery" through the present, nor does it provide a docudrama of the various influences, both social and natural, on the state.[13] This book does include a history of events and individuals from the 1960s to the present with a focus on how they fit within petit-ideology. The mid-1960s constitutes the embarkation point for the study, as that period features a particularly clear divide between the Jeffersonians and Hamiltonians of the state. That political environment is principally examined in the activities of the Republican Party, but Democrats, especially in the 1970s and 1980s, were also prominent within the state at the time and provide an interesting counterbalance to the changes that were occurring in the Republican Party. Those changes were similar to the ones that had been occurring on the national level, with a short lag time.[14]

WHY THIS BOOK IS NEEDED AND WHAT USE IT CAN BE

Studying the political economy of Idaho is a task that various authors seem inspired to tackle every so often. Whether such authors are new residents of the state, novice political observers, politicians, or teachers of state and local politics with a focus on Idaho, the number of sources to be consulted on the state's political ideology and institutions are few and dated. It is my goal with this book to provide many diverse readers—students and experts alike—with a source of information that looks at the state's political environment in a new and provocative manner.

As mentioned above, this book seeks to appeal to a varied readership. With my development of petit-ideology and its foundation in academic work of the past, this book should appeal to scholars in the field of American government, especially those who study state government and politics. Books like this one need to be written because it is important for us to have a collective understanding of the evolution of U.S. state politics. Teachers, principally at the college level in Idaho, should find the book a very useful supplement to other texts, providing as it does a substantive look, grounded in political theory, at aspects of Idaho politics. Lastly, readers who are interested in Idaho politics, including practitioners and political enthusiasts, should find it accessible, even if they are not formally trained in political science.

This book should be a valuable adjunct not only for anyone engaged in intensive study of Idaho's political workings but also for those general readers who want to better understand politics and especially politics in Idaho. That said, this book will probably not please everyone. The scholar may decide it has too many narratives, is not precise enough in places, or does not present adequate "scientific" data and is thus not academic enough. The person who is interested in Idaho politics but does not have academic training in the field may decide that the book has too much theory, or spends too much time on academic studies, or "drags" at times. In trying to create a work that is accessible to a wide spectrum of readers, I undoubtedly have produced a book that will not completely please anyone. But since perfection is impossible, I offer adequacy as a logical fallback.

The first part of the book lays out a foundation for examining the governmental and extragovernmental institutions in Idaho. Chapter 1 aims to provide a framework for the concept of petit-ideology, adapt it to Idaho, and provide that prism for future analyses. Chapter 2 is a concise political history of the state provided for any newcomer or novice to Idaho politics who might want to gain an initial exposure to the state's recent principal figures and events. Those with recollections of or experience with Idaho since the 1960s will see how petit-ideology can be used as a tool for understanding the recent political history of Idaho.

The middle chapters of the book analyzes governmental institutions, including the constitution, of the state. The state constitution is examined to show not only its uniqueness but also, and more prominently, its nature with regard to petit-ideology. The three branches of state government are explored individually in a number of chapters in the manner of most any text covering the state government, but once again petit-ideology is used to supplement the description of each branch to provide an innovative explanation of governmental institutions. Lastly, local governments as they exist in Idaho are scrutinized, showing how small entities supposedly under the control of the state government may, through an individual-focused Jeffersonian vision, attempt to thwart the state's broader Hamiltonian vision.

The final section of the book is an inspection of the extragovernmental institutions found in the state. The ways that interest groups and political parties influence the workings of the constitutional institutions of the state are more understandable through the use of petit-ideology. Petit-ideology reveals the details of relations among the different levels of government and how often an individual's position on the spectrum of petit-ideology changes when one's position in government changes.

An epilogue shows, as does the ultrasound bill discussion above, how petit-ideology can be used to explain a more recent and different policy example. Speculation on the scope of petit-ideology is also considered at the conclusion of the review of Idaho politics and its place in the country. A brief speculation on future areas of exploration, both within and beyond the state of Idaho, conclude this work.

WHY THIS AUTHOR AT THIS TIME

Although there have been a few books on Idaho politics throughout the years, some even exploring the conflicting views of Idahoans, none has approached the subject in terms of petit-ideology, featuring the framework of a continuum from predominance of individual liberty (à la Jefferson) at one end to emphasis on the public good for society as a whole (à la Hamilton) at the other. Moreover, as any teacher of Idaho politics has observed, it has been a long time since the release of any book that even attempts to examine Idaho politics in a systematic and detailed fashion.

While most authors of Idaho politics were probably born and raised in Idaho and may even trace their families to homesteaders, I came to the state later in life. I believe this more detached perspective enables me to view Idaho's society with a foreigner's eye. The most perceptive observer of American politics, Alexis de Tocqueville, was able to see this foreign land with fresh eyes and a realist's mind. Although I cannot compare to Tocqueville in his ability to understand the essence of the society he visited, I do share his wonder of a place that is unfamiliar. Having lived and studied politics in Idaho for more than twenty years, I believe I can share my thoughts and impressions of the people and institutions of the state with others, both native and foreign to Idaho.

IDAHO POLITICS AND GOVERNMENT

CHAPTER ONE

Petit-Ideology

POLITICAL SUBCULTURE RECONSTRUCTED

This chapter develops a theoretical basis for examining the traditional and extragovernmental institutions of the state of Idaho. For nonacademics this chapter may at times seem less captivating than other sections. From a scholarly standpoint the intellectual grounding is necessary for the analysis that follows. Some may thus feel the urge to proceed quickly through the review of theory and prior scholarship. Feel free to do so, but there is much to be gained by understanding the foundation upon which this work is based. Some may find earlier work in the areas of political subculture, ideology, and the beliefs of American founders at least as interesting as what will follow.

POLITICAL SUBCULTURES IN THE AMERICAN STATES

No study of the political environment in the individual states of the nation would be complete without at least a reference to Daniel Elazar and his work on political subcultures. Through the use of immigration and settlement patterns, Elazar created a tripartite system for understanding the political beliefs of citizens in the various states. Although a comprehensive examination of Elazar's work is beyond the scope of this book, a brief survey of the essence of political subcultures is necessary for understanding the evolution from subcultures to the creation of petit-ideology.

Elazar sees political culture as consisting of the underlying attitudes and values present in society and evidenced in the political order.[1] The political culture of a society or nation is not immediately apparent to its citizens, though the culture has a significant influence on the political system of the nation. The political system can never veer too far from the political culture if harmony is to be established and continued.

On the level of individuals political culture circumscribes the political behavior of individuals as well as groups, but political culture cannot be seen as the determinant of behavior itself. Political culture influences the demands that members of society place on the political system, and it defines the political needs of individuals and groups. Wrapped up in the language used in political discourse, political culture orients society toward what it finds to be satisfactory and suggests how it should envision the achievement of political success.

With regard to the United States, Elazar recognizes an overall political culture that is broadly accepted throughout the country, despite each state manifesting its own more distinct orientation toward politics. These subcultures are how the various states focus the national outlook into a more specific influence on populations within the state. The different subcultures are a result of variations in location, demographic streams, and the influence of the national political process within each state.

The American political order is based on two contrasting conceptions of the political world, which Elazar traces back to the founding of the country. In the first view the political order is seen as analogous to a marketplace, with individuals and groups acting out of self-interest and bargaining to achieve political advantage. These individuals and groups look out solely for themselves, and this orientation is seen as both empirical (how society actually operates) and normative (how members of society should act). Political peace is created and maintained through a balance of interests among the participants, whose only common goal is the preservation of the marketplace. No group or individual interest is judged more or less legitimate than others. The second view sees the political order as a commonwealth where citizens cooperate in order to create a situation in which government functions to achieve certain shared moral principles. The commonwealth has not yet been achieved, yet it is the hope of members of society that the ideal commonwealth can be built upon existing political foundations. Participation in government processes in the commonwealth, as compared to the marketplace, is limited to those who conform to the moral principles that are predominant in the polity.

The national culture, influenced by these two views of the political order, is actually a synthesis of three complementary subcultures that have spread across the country, though each still has a locus within a section of the nation. Elazar sees these three subcultures—individualistic, moralistic, and traditionalistic—as the subtext to political life in the United States and the means to understanding political actions and institutions on the subnational level.

The individualistic subculture is the one most influenced by the concept of the democratic order as a marketplace. It emphasizes the centrality of private concerns and limiting community intervention in the activities of the individual. Government intervention is seen as appropriate only in order to keep the marketplace in working order. Adherents of the individualistic subculture believe overall in a very limited regulation of the economy and generally few government initiatives. If government must provide regulations, the regulations should be tailored so all citizens can pursue their own self-interest. The work of politics is seen as a vocation, a livelihood, a profession. The role of the citizen in the individualistic subculture world is principally to vote, with the heavy lifting of politics left to professional politicians. Elazar saw the purest forms of the individualistic subculture in the Middle Atlantic states and the Lower Great Lakes region of the country.

The moralistic subculture type is characterized by the political order being conceived as a commonwealth. Government action is not the necessary evil envisioned within the individualistic subculture but is instead a positive instrument that can assist in the acquisition of moral values dear to the individual members of the community. Government regulates the economy as a means to achieve the common interest even if that entails intervening in the sphere of "private" activities to advance the well-being of the community. The role of the citizen is as a participatory actor. Politics is a public activity that extends beyond merely voting. While more is asked of each individual citizen within the moralistic subculture, more is also asked of politicians formally involved in the political process. Politicians are held to a high level of ethical conduct in both their public and private affairs. One works in politics as a means of public service. Elazar found the moralistic subculture to be dominant in New England and the Upper Midwest.

The traditionalistic subculture is a creature of the southern states, and it shows the strains of the unique history and backdrop of the Confederacy. While ambivalent toward the marketplace, the traditionalistic subculture views the role of government as preserving and reinforcing the power and privileged position of the political elites in society. Government has an active role in the community, but instead of promoting a common interest, as in the moralistic subculture, government in the traditionalistic society favors the status quo and stifles progressive initiatives. Political participation is confined to the elites in society, while others are often not even expected to vote. As in the individualistic subculture, those active in the traditionalistic political realm seek advantage for themselves even if not in the direct pecuniary manner of politicians in the individualistic society. At their magnanimous best, politicians in the traditionalistic sub-culture strive to bolster the status and position of individuals with whom they share social position or family ties. The traditionalistic subculture is rooted in a pre-industrial social order and is losing its influence even in the South of its roots.

POLITICAL SUBCULTURES IN IDAHO

In *American Federalism* Elazar classifies each state into one of eight cate-gories. Those groupings feature either one subculture as singularly dom-inant or one subculture as dominant with a strain of another subculture present. These classifications are determined according to migration and settlement patterns within the states. Elazar groups Idaho with such varied states as California, Washington, New Hampshire, and Iowa, identifying them as "Moralistic Dominant, strong Individualistic strain."[2] A map of the states with the designation of subcultures within their borders indicates that the moralistic subculture is more common in Eastern Idaho and the individualistic strain is strongest in North Idaho.[3] While Elazar may never have set foot in Idaho, most political observers would agree with his general assessment of the state in 1966 and even that his assessment remains sound in the early twenty-first century, although some might quibble and label the state "individualistic dominant, strong moralistic strain." Even Elazar's geographic categorizing of North Idaho as individ-ualistic and Eastern Idaho as moralistic has been endorsed by observers of Idaho politics.[4]

The most extensive study of political culture in Idaho is the work of Robert H. Blank—a monograph published in 1978. Blank of course refers to Elazar in his book, though Blank is not wedded to the Elazar typology, instead leaning more heavily on the work of Donald Devine.[5] Blank attempts to understand the political culture, or subculture, of Idaho according to the state's history and settlement patterns, a method reminiscent of Elazar's approach. In addition to analyzing historical causes, Blank uses public opinion survey data, media reports, and public documents to determine the state of political culture in Idaho. Blank concludes that Idaho's culture is focused on the values of property rights, hard work, and patriotism, all of which can be traced to the early white settlers of the state. Distrust and downright antipathy toward the national government are seen as an outgrowth of the frontier experience. An overall consensus of support for individualistic beliefs is the ultimate finding of Blank's work.[6] He sees Idaho as unique in its subculture but having many commonalities with other Rocky Mountain states.[7]

The tension among inhabitants of the state of Idaho over conflicting values has led researchers to try to geographically isolate the two subcultures within the state. Researchers have sought to add specificity to the generalizations of individualistic North Idaho and moralistic Eastern Idaho. While Blank saw little regional diversity in political and social culture within the state, Leslie Alm et al., again using survey data on public opinion, found significant differences among regions within the state.[8] How one measures and defines political subculture influences the degree of cultural heterogeneity one observes within the state.

The desire to dissect the state of Idaho into homogeneous cultural tidbits seems to be a prevalent pastime of political observers of the state. Randy Stapilus, in his pathbreaking book on the modern history of Idaho politics, provides the reader with a description of distinct regions of the state through the medium of "tours," which are self-contained vignettes of the regions of the state. The state is viewed as comprising four localities: the North Country, the Southwest Valleys, the Middle Mountains, and the Magic Valley.[9]

Stapilus modified his categorization of Idaho into these four distinct regions in a later book on Idaho politics he cowrote with James Weatherby. Weatherby and Stapilus identify four slightly different regions in the state: Northern Idaho, Southwestern Idaho, the Magic Valley, and Eastern Idaho.[10] Maybe due to the state's size, irregular shape, or its particular evolution as a state, no one looks at Idaho as a singular, cohesive polity.

The project to separate Idaho into uniform areas that are islands of consistency unto themselves seems both futile and profligate. No one area, or for that matter no one individual, is a consistent example of a single culture or ideology. It would seem more useful to discover the various and conflicting forces within a society and see how the interaction of those divergent beliefs affects the policies and outputs of the polity. Looking at the mixture of beliefs seems more expedient than attempting to isolate beliefs.

FROM SUBCULTURE TO PETIT-IDEOLOGY

The conflict between the aspirations of individuals and the objectives of society is probably as old as the earliest communities of humankind. Should society allow individuals the freedom to choose their paths to personal fulfillment or should the common interest subsume these private ambitions under the desires of the community? Elazar described this conflict with his marketplace-versus-commonwealth vision of culture, but is culture the only system for understanding this split envisioning of society? Ideology, while similar to culture, encompasses the conception of how people try to understand their society.

Ideology is often seen as a broad understanding of the world that guides the actions of individuals or groups of individuals. Ideology works as a time-saving device. Individuals can use an ideology to more efficiently decide which actions to pursue, instead of having to perform a comprehensive decision-making process whenever faced with a unique situation. An ideology can be seen as an overarching and coherent belief system that assists individuals in making sense of how their world works. Some see ideology as involving questions of power, making it inherently political. Along these lines, ideology is proffered by some as the means by which the dominant group or class in society legitimates its power over others.[11] Ideology in the sense of this study should be seen as political but not the exclusive domain of any dominant or ruling elite.

In order to study the political environment of Idaho, ideology is too broad a concept to be effective. Political values are important to our understanding of the actions of individuals and the formation of institutions in the state, but determining which values should be examined should be of current concern. Culture is also too broad a notion for this exercise. Culture is concerned with the underlying substance of individuals in society, and it forms the basis of broad conceptions of the world and interactions within society. Neither culture nor ideology as they are currently understood suits the needs of a study of the conflicting forces encountered in a particular state of the American nation.

Arising from the work of Elazar, with a touch of the economist Anthony Downs's theories, the concept of petit-ideology takes shape. Instead of looking at ideology with its many contours and levels of measurement, petit-ideology looks at only a single measure of values for an individual, group, or society. Instead of using ambiguous terms that do not have a fixed meaning, such as "liberal" and "conservative," petit-ideology provides a more focused gauge of the attitudes people have about a specific function of government. This new manner of understanding behavior, created specifically for this particular study, complements methods used by others.

Anthony Downs in *An Economic Theory of Democracy* posits a rational basis for aligning public preferences for a bundle of policies along an ideological spectrum that runs from liberal to conservative. Downs uses this mechanism as a means to show how candidates should position their policy stances to maximize the number of votes they get from the electorate.[12] Petit-ideology is a similar continuum between two disparate value dimensions, though it is much narrower than Downs's holistic and ambiguous ideologies. Being a continuum, petit-ideology presents a seemingly infinite number of positions from which one may find an ideal point of satisfaction between two polar opposite extremes of a value. It is not an either/or proposition but a position of a pendulum as it swings along an arc between two poles. A position on the petit-ideological scale is not constant, whether the subject under study is an individual or a society. Changes in an individual or changes in the society can have profound effects on where the pendulum stands at any one point in time.

PETIT-IDEOLOGY AND THE STUDY OF POLITICS IN IDAHO

The use of petit-ideology has many advantages if one is attempting to understand the political environment of a state such as Idaho. Instead of various abstruse measures of policies and institutions, a single concentrated and directed gauge can be used to explain the workings of a complex society. This single measure highlights the paradox of events noted by other observers of Idaho politics. Even among the Rocky Mountain states, Idaho is seen as having natural divisions.[13] Vague terms such as "true conservative," "country club conservative," or "RINO" (i.e., Republican in name only) can be replaced with terms that are centered on a single variable or value. Elazar's subcultures can be refined to allow the observer to concentrate on the values that are of principal influence.

One should not be seduced into believing that the measurement of a single value can answer all pertinent and interesting questions and thus be a "one true empirical love." Single-variable analysis is typically the refuge for the "lovelorn" social scientist who wants a simple answer to all concerns. Petit-ideology is a tool that can assist in observation and discernment, but it is far from the answer to the dreams of the frustrated political analyst.

What then is the petit-ideology that should be used to study Idaho? Elazar notes that the state is conflicted between his subcultures of individualistic and moralistic, the struggle between the marketplace and the commonwealth. That seems like a fruitful place to start. The dichotomy between the individualistic and the communitarian or collectivist attitude has even been used by researchers to determine the level of pathogens in different communities.[14] The question of which values are in opposition is one that involves goals. What should have primacy among the public? Should individuals be placed as the supreme priority, with their interests and desires considered first and foremost when making decisions? Or, should the goals of society, with its collective aspirations, be considered prior to those of the individuals who make up the society? While these goals may not always be in opposition, what does the polity do when there is a clash between the freedom of individuals and the virtuous goals of the commonweal? This is where government comes in. The proper role of government is the logical, normative extension of the tussle between the one and the many. This could be seen as not just *a* question for society but *the* question for society.

If this is the question, what are the poles? What are the two extremes between which an individual, a state, or any collective must fall? Speaking for the side of the primacy of the individual is a long line of voices that stretches at least from Locke and Milton, to Jefferson and Rousseau, to Goldwater and Friedman. The question invokes the concept of liberty, which was what the term "liberal" connoted in its earlier sense, prior to the mid-twentieth century. This sense of liberty and individualism laid the foundation for the belief in democracy, at least democracy in the way it has been envisioned in the United States from Andrew Jackson to the present. Majority rule is seen as a reflection of popular will and the wisdom of individuals to understand their own needs. In this view the role of government, much as in Elazar's individualistic subculture, should be limited and called upon only to protect individual rights, which have often been interpreted as rights to property: provide individuals the latitude to pursue their own desires and wishes while leaving society to flourish through the energy and vigor that such freedom will generate. Society is not an organic entity but basically an amalgamation of free thinking and independently acting beings who combine their energies only when necessary to preserve personal freedom.

The pole that is the extreme for the communitarian side also has a long lineage, spanning from Plato and Cicero, to Hamilton and Burke, to Kennedy and Galbraith. The collective is the most important in this view, and individuals within the collective must subsume their desires for the sake of the common good. This common good is considered a coherent device that is unlike and superior to the sum of the desires of the individuals who make up the community. Related to this view of the greater good is the idea that the majority has no monopoly on this knowledge. Typically the masses, driven by prurient impulses of self-love and greed, are unable to look beyond their petty lives to see what is in the best interests of the whole and in turn in their own best interests. Government is needed to rein in the urges of the population and direct their actions toward more virtuous activity. Democracy, as the term was understood by Plato, is little more than mob rule by the least able in society. Later thinkers have interpreted the modern concept of democracy as that which is reflected in the modern republic. This political system includes a circumscribed position for the public to voice its concerns, with the government having only a limited ability to act on those concerns. Individuals may be equal in their political freedoms but are inherently unequal in their ability to discern the best path for society.

The elite, seen as natural instead of hereditary in modern times, should curb the appetites of the people and direct the machinery of government to pursue the path of virtue, with "ordinary" people having only a limited amount of influence. This influence is necessary so that the governed do not conceive of the system as being tyrannical.

PETIT-IDEOLOGY AS "JEFFERSON VERSUS HAMILTON"

Since terms such as "individualistic," "libertarian," "moralistic," and "communitarian" have been used in many other contexts with varying meanings, their continued use by scholars is confusing and often requires significant effort to clarify how any one author is using the terms. For those who have an interest in politics but lack an academic background, such terms can also become mystifying and have little relationship to the "real" world. Linking famous and well-known figures to petit-ideological positions opens the discussion up to all readers without being condescending to any of them. The problem with using the names of famous individuals in this way is that no individual is a perfect personification of any concept. The convenience of labeling would seem to outweigh the potential complaints that might come from the perfectionist or amateur biographer who would quibble about certain inconsistencies. Such naming conveniences are prevalent in social science, and famous American politicians are a familiar source of labels for political concepts.[15] The use of Jefferson and Hamilton also goes back to Elazar's interpretation that the overall political order of the United States consists of two contrasting conceptions of the political world that can be traced to the founding of the nation.[16]

For the side of the petit-ideology arc that identifies the individual as the most important element of society, Thomas Jefferson makes for a logical standard-bearer.[17] The principal author of the Declaration of Independence put his faith in the ability of the "common man" to discern his own best interests without government guidance or assistance from the parts of society deemed by some as more capable of making decisions for the community. Jefferson viewed people as naturally amicable, warm-hearted, and benevolent and thus best served by small, unobtrusive government. In a classic liberal understanding of society, government, especially government that is not close to the people, would restrict individual liberty and prevent the common people of the land from achieving their potential. The individual thus comes before community. In this view, allowing all members of the community to have the greatest possible latitude in exercising their self-evident rights and liberties produces the best outcomes for society as a whole.[18]

Jefferson, like anyone else, was not consistent in his beliefs, and his actions did not always reflect his stated values. His prejudices against nonwhite persons and women are well documented and were manifest in his actions. Liberty and freedom of action were, in Jefferson's mind, reserved exclusively for men such as himself. Jefferson did not live the life of the yeoman farmer but instead spent extravagantly and relied on a sizable slave population to keep him comfortable. Even in his political actions Jefferson could stray far from his stated beliefs. Whether it was support for foreign powers or the acquisition of Louisiana in a purchase even he thought to be beyond the bounds of the Constitution, Jefferson, like many others, allowed expediency to override ideological fealty. Despite such shortcomings, Jefferson, especially considering his place in the pantheon of American deities of liberty, seems to be the logical choice to name the individualistic side of petit-ideology.

For the polar opposite of Jefferson, there is little choice other than Jefferson's archrival, Alexander Hamilton.[19] Hamilton was the principal defender of the Constitution during the ratification fight, though he did not contribute much to the actual drafting of the document despite being a delegate to the constitutional convention. Hamilton viewed humans as driven by ambition, avarice, and an insatiable lust for preeminence. He thought that these selfish propensities, especially those of "common" men, needed to be controlled to assure social stability. Only through a strong central government dominated by a natural elite, with prominence based on talent rather than birthright, could society overcome the inherent cupidity of the masses. Reducing individual independence, according to Hamilton, would limit the chances of civil disorder.[20] This robust national government should be dominated by the executive and judiciary branches, which would provide a check on the more popularly influenced legislature. Hamilton believed that the Constitution was too timid in its safeguards against runaway "democracy," and he spoke openly during the convention of a love for a British-style government complete with a monarch. The typical individual was so craven with lust for personal advancement that only a learned and virtuous elite could be trusted with the levers of power. While Jefferson placed his faith in the ordinary man, Hamilton believed in the need for an extraordinary man.

Like Jefferson, Hamilton had many faults, though he did seem more consistent in matching his actions with his beliefs and remedies for the ills of society. If anything, Hamilton's private life exemplified his under-standing of the motives of human action. He was vain, salacious in his private life, and overly ambitious in his public desire for power and influ-ence. Hamilton could be petty and vengeful in his actions and expressions toward others, especially his political rivals. In his political musings and actions, Hamilton consistently looked to aggrandize the influence of the executive branch within the national government while supporting the financial and mercantile sections of the economy. Again, far from a perfect model for the communitarian pole of our continuum, Hamilton fits the bill better than any other actor of the founding generation.

USING PETIT-IDEOLOGY TO STUDY IDAHO POLITICS

Petit-ideology provides many advantages when evaluating politics in general and politics in Idaho in particular. Although political culture and specifically the scholarship on political subcultures have been used extensively, few new applications have been developed. Researchers are still using political subcultures based on ancestry and migratory patterns and trying to place specific subcultures in geographic areas.[21] Petit-ideology provides a dynamic new tool that can be used by polit-ical observers to better understand policies, institutions, and general political behavior.

The primacy of ideology as an explanation for political institutions and behavior has been questioned, and with good reason. Through extensive analysis, researchers such as Christopher Achen and Larry Bartels have argued that ideology and rational congruence of beliefs have little util-ity in explaining political actors, especially when the discussion turns to elections.[22] Voters are partisans who shape their preferences according to their preferred political party. Achen and Bartels indicate in their extensive study that election outcomes have little to do with ideology and rationality and instead depend almost exclusively on the mobilization of voters. This would seem to devalue the importance of petit-ideology as a method for understanding political behavior.

Such an argument might be relevant elsewhere, and I am not going to refute it here, but partisanship has little currency in a one-party state such as Idaho. When Republicans dominate a supermajority of state legislative districts and when all state offices are held by the GOP, the real electoral contests are the primaries, where no partisan cues are available. While partisanship is as vibrant in Idaho as in other states, as researchers have observed, it cannot be used to understand the conflict in Idaho, as was seen in the initial example with the ultrasound legislation. In Idaho, which is the subject of this book, petit-ideology provides a method for understanding intraparty differences.

Petit-ideology is also superior to typologies used in colloquial conversations outside of academia. As this book attempts to be open to readers who are political practitioners and observers outside of academia, tools that help everyone better classify policies, institutions, and even individuals would be beneficial. Ideological terms such as "liberal" and "conservative" have been so contorted in contemporary discourse as to be almost completely incomprehensible. Many now try to further categorize positions by using circuitous terms. Among just "conservatives" titles can include "true conservative," "social conservative," "fiscal conservative," "cultural conservative," "paleo-conservative," and "fauxcons." Petit-ideology's use of a spectrum based on clear visions of the primacy of outlook (the individual versus society) adds clarity in assigning labels to policies, institutions, and individuals. Linking petit-ideology with two prominent founders of the country allows political observers of all stripes to understand the concept.

Petit-ideology may be used as a barometer by which to evaluate institutions and individuals in the political world of Idaho. As Idaho has been described by some as a paradox that seems to struggle with an identity that lies between two opposing visions of what society should value and to what degree it should value them, petit-ideology can inform the researcher as to where along the continuum of views the element under study can be located. Portions of both formal and informal organizations in government can be studied to see how their functions and creation reflect petit-ideology. People can be analyzed to see how their actions and political positions fall along the arc of petit-ideology. The remainder of this book uses this instrument to analyze the recent political history of Idaho, especially the participants and the institutions of Idaho state politics, both formal branches of government and extragovernmental entities such as political parties and interest groups. While petit-ideology will be a focus of this investigation, its use is secondary to providing a new perspective and perception of Idaho.

CHAPTER TWO

Petit-Ideology in Idaho

THE RISE OF THE JEFFERSONIANS AND HAMILTONIANS

In order to provide a suitable foundation for examining the institutions and policies of government in the state of Idaho, an abbreviated history of the recent political past seems necessary. This narrative, like most, proceeds in chronological order with only slight deviations to assure continuity, and it concentrates on political giants. Despite its relatively small size, Idaho has had more than its share of larger-than-life figures in the political world. From the early twentieth century, and thus before the period covered here, the lineup includes Moses Alexander, the country's first Jewish governor; Glen Taylor, U.S. senator and vice presidential candidate on the Progressive ticket in 1948; and of course Sen. William Borah.[1] The prominent figures in Idaho politics from the middle of the last century to the beginning of the current century are examined, including their backgrounds, beliefs, and policy preferences. Sources for this examination include background from personal memoirs to enhance secondary sources on specific politicians and Idaho in general. Petit-ideology provides the basis for gaining an understanding of the people and politics of the time, with the continuum from Jefferson to Hamilton serving as a framework on which to place figures and positions in comparable stead. This chronology also shows that success often comes not by tacking to the extremes of petit-ideology but by finding a calm harbor in the middle. A new place in petit-ideology, one that is a moderate stance or median between Jefferson and Hamilton, is ascertained and named after another founding father, one who is less well known but who was situated at the pragmatic center that best describes the most effective political figures in Idaho.

As governors often are emblematic of how the populace in Idaho sees itself, the chief executive dominates this whirlwind history. A short interlude on two senators who might best exemplify the opposite poles of petit-ideology adds variety to the story. Also, a concise look at James Wilson, who constitutes the petit-ideology median position, serves to complete the cast of characters who represent the principal positions on the petit-ideology spectrum.

GOV. ROBERT SMYLIE: FIRST AND LAST HAMILTONIAN

Modern political history in Idaho begins with Robert Smylie.[2] Although Smylie himself saw his predecessor in the governorship, C. A. Robins, as being the man who brought Idaho government into the twentieth century, it was Smylie who changed the state government into a force that would affect the lives of Idahoans to a greater extent than it had in the past.

Although born in Iowa, Smylie traveled—hitchhiked—to Idaho to visit relatives and eventually enrolled at the College of Idaho. He played football and worked odd jobs to pay his way through school. These experiences during the Depression had a significant effect on Smylie and help explain his later view of the need for more of a collective sense of society.

The future governor took a route common to many who desire power through government. Smylie completed his law degree at George Washington University before returning to Idaho to work in the Office of the Attorney General. With the death of the incumbent officeholder, Smylie was elevated to the statewide position before winning the office in his own right in 1950. He would move from the attorney general's office to the governor's office just down the hall after the 1954 election.

At this time Smylie, similar to Hamilton, started to feel the desire to exercise greater power. Smylie, musing about the reason for his decision to run for governor in 1954, noted the desire for power clearly: "Most of the time you could almost hear the hum of those wheels of power, and, if you listened very closely, you could sometimes hear them whir when they got out of gear. I think it was the knowledge of all of that power just forty feet away that finally led me . . . to try and get my hands on those levers and learn how to run that power for the benefit of the people of the state."[3] Also similar to Hamilton, Smylie believed that government had a positive purpose: to influence the lives of its citizens. "I had an unquenchable thirst to start doing the things for Idaho that I thought needed doing in the field of education (both public school and higher education), in the manner of highway transportation, in economic development, and in the development of a system of parks and recreation," he wrote.[4] Most of these areas were not seen at the time as the purview of government, and some, especially economic development, represent strictly Hamiltonian visions of the role of government.

As governor, Smylie expanded the role of government in Idaho into many facets of the lives of his constituents. Besides the areas mentioned above, Smylie also created the Department of Commerce, the Idaho State Historical Society Museum, the Department of Water Resources, and the Permanent Building Fund. This expansion of government paled in comparison with his work to enlarge the role of the state government in regard to education.

Governor Smylie began his term by "fully funding" the public schools in the state. This funding amount was dictated by a formula for public school equalization that had not been met in the past. Education and its funding would become Smylie's first and last acts as governor.

Smylie was looking for broader horizons after having been elected for his unprecedented third term in 1962. When Henry Dworshak, a U.S. senator from Idaho, died in 1962, Smylie considered appointing himself to the position but instead decided on former governor Len Jordan, whom Smylie believed would not run for another term, leaving the Senate position to Smylie in 1966. Smylie was even considered as a potential running mate for Nelson Rockefeller if the New York governor had won the Republican Party's nomination for president in 1964. But with Barry Goldwater's ascendancy in the GOP, Smylie's future was truncated at both the national level and eventually in Idaho as well.

In 1965, in what some pundits have called the most momentous state legislative session in Idaho history, a sales tax was approved for the stated purpose of providing revenue for public schools, especially during economic downturns.[5] One caveat about the proposed tax was that, besides needing to be passed by the state legislature, the levy needed to be approved by a referendum of the voters in November 1966. This is an example of the Hamiltonian vision of the public good of education being tempered by the belief in the individual, as espoused by Jefferson. The referendum passed, with Governor Smylie being one of the principal proponents of the tax. Smylie's support of taxes, along with his other Hamiltonian actions as governor, would contribute to his downfall.

Not wanting to challenge Jordan for the U.S. Senate and with no other federal position open to him, in 1966 Smylie began his fourth run for the governor's office. Although some, including Smylie himself, believed the governor was overconfident and had overstayed his welcome in the office, the shift of the Republican Party on both the state and national level from the Hamiltonian side of petit-ideology to the Jeffersonian side should not be overlooked as a significant reason for the termination of Smylie's political career.

DON SAMUELSON AND RISE OF THE JEFFERSONIANS

The year 1964 and the nomination of Barry Goldwater for president constituted both the zenith and the nadir for the Jeffersonians in the national political galaxy. The takeover of the Republican Party apparatus by Goldwater supporters was short-lived, and Jeffersonians would not gain ascendancy nationally again until Ronald Reagan's election. Similar to many trends, the rise of the Jeffersonians was delayed in Idaho, though Goldwater almost carried the state in the 1964 general election.

After Goldwater's loss, Smylie, with the assistance of other Hamiltonian-leaning governors, effected both a purge of Goldwater Jeffersonians from the Republican National Committee and the creation of the policy-driven Republican Coordinating Committee (RCC) to generate position papers.[6] Smylie's activities piqued the John Birch Society (JBS). Smylie, with future president Gerald Ford, pushed the RCC to condemn the JBS and urge Republicans not to join the Jeffersonian group.[7] Smylie's actions contributed significantly to his eventual downfall.

The Jeffersonians in Idaho needed a standard-bearer, and they found one in a gunsmith from the North Idaho town of Sandpoint. Don Samuelson was elected to the state senate in 1960 after a failed attempt for a house seat two years earlier.[8] As state senator, Samuelson supported the elimination of S&H Green Stamps, a twentieth-century grocery store rewards program, and the passage of a "right-to-work" law in the state.

Although not mentioned prominently in Samuelson's writings, Smylie's support for the sales tax was an albatross that Samuelson could exploit without even having to mention the issue.

Sensing that Smylie could not win the general election in 1966 and finding no other Republican willing to challenge the sitting governor, Samuelson decided to run himself, even though he had no animus toward Smylie. Running a low-profile campaign with implicit support from the JBS, Samuelson triumphed in the Republican primary in a landslide over Smylie, defeating the longest-serving governor in Idaho history up to that time.

The general election for governor of Idaho in 1966 had more twists and turns than old U.S. Highway 95 at White Bird Hill. The original Democratic nominee, Charles Herndon, died in a plane crash in September. The Democratic Central Committee had to find a replacement for Herndon, and with the help of Sen. Frank Church (more on him later), a state senator from North Idaho named Cecil Andrus was nominated with no votes to spare. Two independents had jumped into the race before Herndon's plane crash: Perry Swisher, a supporter of the sales tax, spurred to run due to Herndon's indifference to the tax and Samuelson's vote against it; and Phillip Jungert, who favored laws to permit gambling. With the two independents garnering more than 20 percent of the vote, Samuelson was able to squeak by Andrus despite receiving only 41 percent of the vote.[9] Samuelson, with his dedication to limited government and belief in individual initiative, would lead Idaho for the next four years.

Don Samuelson had a controversial term as governor. Hounded by the press and uncomfortable in formal settings, Samuelson was ridiculed by some as stupid—"Big Dumb Don"—while lionized by others as friendly, down-to-earth, and bluntly honest.[10] True to his Jeffersonian roots, the governor felt that his common touch was virtuous, and he shunned professional elites in favor of his own style of common sense. Whether it was reading a bill passed by the legislature word for word or threatening to veto bills that had not passed yet, Samuelson was a complex political figure despite being seen as simple. Samuelson was consistent in his values yet struggled turning those values into governing principles. A Jeffersonian governor in the twenty-first century would have better luck at governing the state.

Samuelson's brand of Jeffersonian individualism had become predominant in the Idaho Republican Party, and the Hamiltonians were a shrinking minority in the state. Only a political figure who straddled the abyss between Hamilton and Jefferson could wrest control away from the ascendant Jeffersonians. Before examining this Idaho politico, we must return to the country's founding to discover the precedent for occupying the "sweet spot" on the petit-ideology spectrum.

JAMES WILSON: THE PETIT-IDEOLOGY MEDIAN

James Wilson was instrumental in the founding of the nation, yet there has been little written about him.[11] Born in Scotland, Wilson immigrated to America and eventually sought out a career in the law. His career was sidetracked by the growing tension with Britain. Wilson would be influential in forging independence and creating the Constitution. Some see Wilson as the most underrated founder and argue that his influence on the Constitution was second only to Madison's.[12]

Wilson was chosen by the Pennsylvania Assembly to be a delegate to the Second Continental Congress in 1775. He served on numerous committees and was described as being, along with George Washington and John Jay, part of the moderate force in the forum between the conservatives, such as Wilson's mentor John Dickerson (who wanted to preserve the union with Britain), and the radicals, such as John Adams (who wanted to be completely independent of Britain).[13] Wilson was not just a moderating influence; he was called upon to forge compromises in various situations. His skill for compromise was tested when Wilson was sent to western Pennsylvania to negotiate a treaty with native tribes, many of whom were antagonistic to the rebels and each other.

As 1776 began, the Continental Congress was being prodded by the radicals, mostly from Massachusetts and Virginia, to make a formal break with the mother country. Although the country and delegates were nearly unanimous in their disdain toward Parliament, a sizable faction was still loyal to the king. Wilson worked to stall a decision to call for independence until public sentiment was more unified behind the break with Britain. When the mood of the general population swung toward independence as 1776 reached its midpoint, Wilson persuaded his Pennsylvania colleague Dickerson to abstain from voting so the colony could unanimously support the Declaration of Independence. Eventually even the radical Adams saw the wisdom of delay to ensure that Congress did not get in front of public support.[14] Wilson would go on to sign the Declaration of Independence.

By 1786 Wilson was seeing the need for a stronger union to replace the system created under the Articles of Confederation, and he was chosen to attend the constitutional convention the following year. Wilson's beliefs as expressed during the convention did not fall entirely on either the Jeffersonian or the Hamiltonian side of petit-ideology. He favored the direct election of both chambers of the legislature and the executive, showing his belief in the people à la Jefferson. In contrast to Jefferson, however, Wilson favored a single vibrant executive who, along with the judiciary, should be given the power of an absolute veto over acts of the legislature, à la Hamilton.

Wilson was so trusted among his colleagues that Benjamin Franklin had Wilson deliver a speech for the elderly statesman when Franklin's voice faltered. He was also chosen to serve on the Committee of Detail, which created compromises between conflicting resolutions passed by the assembly. But it was his art for finding the happy median in a dispute that had the greatest effect on the Constitution. Although a northern delegate who had had little experience with slavery, James Wilson is credited (or damned) as the person who came up with the Three-Fifths Compromise that determined apportionment of representatives in the House. Wilson was pragmatic enough to put aside ideology in order to develop a plan acceptable to the convention.

After the signing of the Constitution, the speech James Wilson made outside the Pennsylvania State House—now Independence Hall—was the first and most comprehensive argument in favor of ratifying the newly written Constitution. While the more famous *Federalist Papers* went into more depth on myriad issues, Wilson's speech, which was later reprinted widely, provided a cogent defense of the overall structure and purpose of the new government while countering claims by detractors concerning the absence of a bill of rights, the potential oppression by a standing army, and the aristocratic nature of the Senate. Wilson acknowledged that there were aspects of the Constitution he wished were different, but he also believed that nothing closer to perfection could have been accomplished at the convention.

So how does Wilson fit into petit-ideology? Like James Wilson, the Wilsonian position in the petit-ideology framework has strong opinions yet does not allow those views to preclude working toward a pragmatic solution to political problems. The Wilsonian is a practical evaluator of what is possible instead of a dogmatic fanatic who loses the crumb for the sake of the loaf. The point is not that Jeffersonians and Hamiltonians do not ever compromise their values to achieve a partial goal; it is that the Wilsonian consistently puts accomplishment before moral purity. The Wilsonian is not amoral, but this position permits seeing the value of both the individual and society. Being more democratic than Hamilton and more virtuous than Jefferson, Wilson was able to find compromise between the extreme positions of the others.

While all public figures, institutions, and policies have aspects of both Hamilton and Jefferson, they also all borrow a tad from Wilson. The value of the model is to identify where the "sweet spot" can be found on the petit-ideology arc. While all politicians may believe they tack toward the center, some have a natural ability to find the Wilsonian equilibrium point. Voters, especially in Idaho since the 1960s, have warmly rewarded the Wilsonians who seek office.

CECIL ANDRUS: THE CONSUMMATE WILSONIAN

Cecil Andrus has been described by some as Idaho's greatest governor.[15] While many would disagree with this ranking, Andrus certainly was popular. He was elected governor four separate times, with the first and last elections twenty years apart. Andrus provides an example of the political figure who believes in the value of compromise, though he preferred to use the term "hornswoggling."[16] His political life shows the Wilsonian model in its best light with a distinct Idahoan tint.

Andrus was born in Oregon, served in the Korean War, and then moved to Idaho to work as a logger and mill manager in Orofino. According to Andrus himself, he entered politics because of a slight by a Republican state senator, or from listening to a speech by John Kennedy, or in order to improve education for his daughter and other young people in rural Idaho.[17] As a state senator, Andrus focused primarily on education issues, including the revision of the formula for the allocation of state aid to local school districts. He was also one of the only Democrats from North Idaho to support the state sales tax, which was ostensibly intended to support primary education.[18] Working with Republicans and Eastern Idaho legislators who leaned more to the Hamiltonian side of petit-ideology, Andrus often veered from the positions of the Jeffersonian Democrats of North Idaho.

In a rematch with Samuelson in 1970 Andrus won the governorship by a narrow margin. The campaign was based on showing Andrus as the centrist Wilsonian and Samuelson as the extremist Jeffersonian. Using the slogan "A Governor for ALL Idaho" and stressing moderate "quality of life" issues, Andrus was able to find the median in Idaho's petit-ideology. This is not to say that the Wilsonian position was favored by the vast majority of Idaho voters. By winning 52 percent of the vote, Andrus illustrated how a candidate could find a middle position to overcome Idaho's predominantly Jeffersonian leanings in the middle of the twentieth century.

Andrus's tenure as governor, which actually covered two separate periods, 1971–77 and 1987–95, highlighted many issues that exemplified his Wilsonian compromise approach. In his own words Andrus was not an environmentalist but a conservationist. Public land was to be preserved, not to protect endangered species but to allow Idahoans to recreate in the outdoors. If the government protected wilderness areas that conserved the ability for people to hunt, fish, camp, and experience nature *and* saved endangered species, then Andrus could be supported by voters of various stripes.[19] Where Samuelson the Jeffersonian supported mining in the White Cloud Mountains as confirmation of an unimpeded marketplace, Andrus favored protecting the scenic area for the use of the community—in the Hamiltonian sense—but also for free individuals to pursue their outdoor passions—in the Jeffersonian sense. Andrus sought solutions that would thread the policy needle.

In another environmental issue—nuclear waste—Andrus again found the happy median in petit-ideology. When the national government attempted to send waste from U.S. Navy activities to Idaho in amounts beyond what had been agreed to, Andrus had a state trooper stand on the railroad tracks to block the delivery.[20] Again he was able to find an issue that was appealing to the majority along the petit-ideology spectrum. Those against nuclear power were joined in supporting Andrus by those who opposed the national government imposing its will on the state. Few in Idaho fought Andrus in this highly visible dispute.

Andrus was even able to find a middle ground on abortion. In 1990, an election year for the governor and state legislature, a bill to severely restrict abortion was passed by the legislature after being introduced to Idaho by pro-life groups from out of state. Idaho, as would be seen with the ultrasound bill in 2012, was viewed by the rest of the country as ripe for legislation to roll back *Roe v. Wade*. Andrus vetoed the bill despite being against abortion personally, at least partially due to his Catholic faith. Andrus felt that, though there were passionate advocates on both sides of the issue (i.e., Jeffersonians and Hamiltonians), a majority of people were ambivalent on the issue of terminating pregnancies. He saw the majority as uncomfortable with the extremists and did not feel this personal issue should be dealt with by the government.[21] Presenting himself as personally against abortion, like a good Hamiltonian, while insisting on the sanctity of the individual to act without the interference of the government, like a good Jeffersonian, Andrus was showing consummate Wilsonian skills.

Being a Wilsonian was also obviously politically successful. Although he only barely beat Samuelson in 1970 and did not even get a majority of the vote in beating David Leroy in 1986, Andrus did win four gubernatorial races that stretched over three decades. Regardless, Cecil Andrus showed how a Wilsonian politician could be successful in Idaho, a fact not lost on future officeholders.

CHURCH AND SYMMS'S HAMILTONIAN/JEFFERSONIAN CLASH

As a U.S. senator, Frank Church was seen as the heir to William Borah, as both men followed issues that went beyond Idaho and focused on society rather than the individual. Although Church can be seen as a champion of individual rights with the work of the Church Committee, which investigated abuses by the intelligence community relating to American citizens' political activism, from his earliest days he sought to pursue expansive issues. Senator Church was clearly a Hamiltonian, though his positions may have led to his defeat in 1980.

Church was fascinated with politics at a young age.[22] After marrying the daughter of a former governor, running unsuccessfully for the state legislature at age twenty-eight, and helping other young veterans take over the Ada County Democratic organization, Church made the leap to running for the U.S. Senate. After winning the Democratic primary over the eccentric Glen Taylor by 170 votes, a victory Taylor contended involved electoral shenanigans, Church beat the incumbent Republican Herman Welker by a large margin, thus becoming a U.S. senator at the age of thirty-two.

Upon reaching the Senate, Church attempted to emulate his idol Borah, with whom he shared great oratory skills, by requesting to be on the Senate Foreign Relations Committee. Soon after his arrival, Church voted against Lyndon Johnson, the all-powerful majority leader in the Senate, on a tabling motion concerning civil rights legislation before the Senate. Johnson tossed his pen to the floor and placed Church into senatorial purgatory. Barred from Foreign Relations and on the outs with Johnson, Frank Church used his keen legal mind to create an amendment to the civil rights bill to assure its eventual passage. The grateful Johnson granted absolution to Church, which included a seat on the Foreign Relations Committee, where he would gain fame in the future. Church was seen as not having a visceral interest in civil rights; his interest was more intellectual.[23] He was a lawmaker who would be heralded by those with a Hamiltonian view of the world.

Church's career in the Senate focused on national issues that were Hamiltonian in scope. He was an early critic of the Vietnam War and pressed for expansion of environmental protections, including the River of No Return Wilderness area that now bears his name. Church is probably best remembered for being chair of a select committee that investigated the FBI and CIA for extralegal activities. His committee work kept him from beginning his campaign for president in 1976 until it was too late to derail Jimmy Carter's nomination. Although Church supported some issues that could be seen as Jeffersonian, such as opposition to gun control laws, he was overwhelmingly a Hamiltonian. These positions left him open to attacks from the opposite side of the petit-ideology spectrum.

Steve Symms, in a manner similar to that of Church, began his political career by running for the U.S. Congress, though Symms began with a House race in 1972.[24] A natural campaigner, Symms professed a Jeffersonian individualism that seemed embedded in his native Canyon County. The year 1972 featured electoral triumphs for Republicans throughout the country but not for Hamiltonian Republicans in Idaho. Symms breezed to victory in his primary, while former governor Smylie lost his bid to be elected to the Senate to future senator Jim McClure, who was much closer to Symms than Smylie. This election propelled Symms into politics and started a surge of Jeffersonian fervor in Idaho.

While Symms was trying to make a mark in the House, a Jeffersonian colleague, Robert Smith, ran against Frank Church in 1974. Smith had run Symms's 1972 campaign and initially worked on Symms's staff in Washington. Smith pushed Jeffersonian themes but was tarnished by associations with the JBS, an organization that did not fit in with the Canyon County Jeffersonians. Smith lost to Church but showed that the senator could be beaten but not by a pure Jeffersonian. Church was also helped by the strong Democratic tide of 1974 in the wake of Watergate and the resignation of Richard Nixon from the presidency.[25]

Through the 1970s Symms began to mix his extreme Jeffersonian views with a Hamiltonian touch. He began to be less strident and started to follow more closely the Wilsonian Jim McClure.[26] This shift can be seen in Symms's change from his original Jeffersonian pro-choice position on abortion to a pro-life approach. This "move to the middle" allowed Symms to be more palatable to a statewide audience that was less Jeffersonian than the First Congressional District, which included the individualistic strongholds of his native Canyon County and North Idaho. Symms had to become acceptable to Hamiltonian Eastern Idaho, which Daniel Elazar had characterized as the moralistic section of Idaho.

By 1980 Church had begun to look like his Hamiltonian—yet Republican—predecessor, Robert Smylie.[27] Church was characterized as out of touch, arrogant, and having served too long—the same barbs that had been directed at Smylie in 1966. Senator Church was also too Hamiltonian, especially as Idaho and the nation were becoming more Jeffersonian. Symms, the gregarious campaigner, was a natural "Robin" to Ronald Reagan's "Batman" in 1980 Idaho. Idaho and the nation were ready to move farther along the petit-ideology spectrum toward the Jeffersonian pole.

Church's campaign was lackluster, and even the champion debater could do no better than a draw with Symms, who practiced extensively. While Church spoke formally in towns throughout the state, Symms used a family RV and bus to make grand entrances and spur high-energy appearances.

But probably the most influential factor in the 1980 senatorial campaign was the intervention of groups separate from the formal, official campaigns. The Anybody-But-Church group, abortion activists, environmental groups, and opponents of Church's support for the Panama Canal treaty energized and nationalized the campaign. Church was also targeted by the National Conservative Political Action Committee along with six other Democratic senators. Even with those tailwinds easing his campaign on the coattails of Ronald Reagan's run for the presidency, Symms beat Church by less than 1 percent of the vote.

Frank Church would die of pancreatic cancer less than four years after losing his Senate seat. Steve Symms would serve two terms in the Senate, with few legislative accomplishments to his name. Symms seemed to thrive on controversy, and when he left the Senate he became a lobbyist.

PHIL BATT: THE WILSONIAN REPUBLICAN

Phil Batt was involved in the governance of Idaho in many roles for almost thirty-five years. It would be difficult to be so successful and influential without being Wilsonian. Growing up on a farm in rural Wilder, Batt would have an unpretentious career that was known more for his policy accomplishments than his political positions.[28]

Batt's political career started in the 1965 state legislative session, which he called historic. With the sales tax for education, reform of the judiciary, and redistricting to get the state legislature into conformity with the rulings of the Supreme Court of the United States, that legislative term was very productive. After his one term in the lower chamber of the legislature, Batt would go on to serve more than a decade in the state senate, including eight years as majority leader and two as president pro tempore. Batt won his race for lieutenant governor in 1978, only to lose his gambit for governor to the incumbent, John Evans, four years later. After a return to the state senate and a stint on the state transportation board, Batt was named state Republican Party chair after an impressive showing by the Democrats in both legislative and statewide races in 1990. Batt worked feverishly to rebuild the Republican grassroots organization in every county of the state. This organization would bode well for Batt's future, as he won the gubernatorial election in 1994 against an initially favored Democrat and sitting state attorney general, Larry

Echo Hawk. Running an almost flawless campaign that was helped by an inept Echo Hawk operation and a formidable national Republican tide, Batt won rather easily. Since Batt's reorganization of the state party, the Republicans in Idaho have lost only one U.S. House seat among national government posts and only the state superintendent of education among statewide offices.

As governor, Batt showed himself to be a pragmatic Wilsonian. He had roots in Canyon County, the bastion of Jeffersonian individualism, but Batt governed more in the Hamiltonian manner. Before, after, and even during his political career, Batt was an independent-minded onion farmer. Even into the 1990s farmworkers in Idaho were not covered under any form of workers' compensation insurance. Bucking many of his Jeffersonian friends who thought the government should not interfere in private agreements between farmers and their workers, Batt pushed a farmworkers' compensation law through the state legislature. According to Batt, this was the only issue during his term as governor where he personally lobbied members of legislature. He recognized his support of rights for farmworkers to have cost him friends, but, in classic Wilsonian fashion, he considered it the right thing to do.[29]

Batt and Andrus, the Democratic Wilsonian, had a friendship that overcame partisan differences and led to both men working together on policy issues. The most prominent issue of convergence for the two governors was the storage of nuclear waste in Idaho. Andrus had fought the national government on this issue during his tenure in office, including filing a lawsuit, while Batt worked to develop a long-term solution to the problem. The result of Batt's work was a complex agreement that would reduce shipments to the state and eventually remove all waste in the coming decades. Although there were many who thought the deal did not go far enough, a referendum to undo the agreement was defeated at the ballot box.[30] When a subsequent governor tried to amend the agreement, Andrus and Batt together chastised the plan in the media.

Batt and Andrus, though often differentiated from each other on partisan and ideological bases, are actually quite similar on the basis of petit-ideology. Both former governors sought to achieve pragmatic solutions to what seemed intractable problems by adhering to principles that borrowed from both the Jeffersonian and Hamiltonian sides of petit-ideology.

C. L. "BUTCH" OTTER: A JEFFERSONIAN GOVERNING
AS A WILSONIAN

C. L. "Butch" Otter was born into the same Jeffersonian world of Canyon County as Steve Symms. While Symms moved away from the Jeffersonian pole of petit-ideology during his legislative career, Otter retained his individualistic outlook on the world until he was elected to govern the entire state of Idaho.

Otter was from Caldwell and graduated from the College of Idaho in 1967. He parlayed his political science degree into an entry-level position at the J. R. Simplot Company, where Otter rose through the ranks and married the owner's daughter. His political career started early; in 1972 Otter was elected to the first of two terms in the state house of representatives.[31]

The Jeffersonian orientation of Otter was evident early in his legislative career when he voted against an antipornography bill (Otter was noted to have answered the roll call vote with "Hell no") and even questioning the illegality of marijuana.[32] Such extreme positions did not sit well even with many Republican voters, and Otter came in a distant third in the GOP primary for governor in 1978. This loss kept him out of elected office for almost a decade.

Butch Otter returned to politics in 1986 in a race for lieutenant governor rather than the top executive post; the governor's race that year pitted Andrus against Republican David Leroy. Otter would remain in the second position in the state government for fourteen years, including after the 1990 election, when Otter had to break a tie in an organizational vote between the even number of Republicans and Democrats in the state senate to retain the GOP's majority in the chamber. The only other memorable event during Otter's tenure as lieutenant governor was his arrest for drunk driving. Even after providing numerous and curious excuses for his condition after being pulled over on the highway, Otter went on to win subsequent elections in Idaho. His conviction probably did deter Otter from running for governor in 1994.

During his fourth term as lieutenant governor, Otter chose to run for the open seat in Idaho's First Congressional District. With the district's Jeffersonian-leaning Canyon County and North Idaho, Otter easily won election over a tepid Democratic challenge. Congress proved a lonely place for Otter's Jeffersonian views, however. After the attacks of September 11,

2001, Otter was one of only three Republicans to vote against the USA PATRIOT Act. He consistently fought against various programs that sought to expand surveillance, including a provision to collect information on book buyers and library users. Otter's colleague in the fight supporting readers' rights was Bernie Sanders, the socialist Jeffersonian from Vermont.

Otter served three terms in Congress before finally reaching the governor's office he had been seeking for almost thirty years. Three easy elections made Otter another longtime resident of the Idaho governor's office. Since moving into the second floor of the capitol, Governor Otter has also moved away from the Jeffersonian extreme of petit-ideology.

Otter's Catholic upbringing may have been a factor in pulling him away from his once overwhelmingly Jeffersonian outlook. He has been consistently against abortion and same-sex marriage. He has often explained these positions, as well as others he has taken while governor, through reference to the Idaho constitution or laws passed by the state legislature. Otter's positions as governor may have moved toward the Wilsonian center of petit-ideology in order for him to better govern the state and to better express his religious views in the political context.

Otter has shown a greater predilection toward the Wilsonian position with a number of issues during his tenure as governor of Idaho. The Affordable Care Act offered one example of how Otter can balance his beliefs against the need to govern. While the governor has railed against the act and even signed an executive order prohibiting state agencies from complying with it, Otter was pragmatic enough, in a Wilsonian sense, to push for the construction of a state health-care exchange as the best solution for Idahoans. In the areas of highway construction, taxes, and education Otter saw the legislature reject his initial proposals. Rather than dogmatically insisting on his positions, Otter would often compromise with the state legislature when possible. He also learned that more input from the public, especially concerning education, can lead to greater success after education reform bills he supported were overturned by voters in a referendum.

Despite his long and sometimes convoluted journey through Idaho politics, Otter is one of the most electorally successful individuals in the history of the state. Being able to become more Wilsonian has certainly helped him, as it has other successful politicians in Idaho. A later chapter discusses how an individual's changing positions within government (e.g., moving from the legislative to the executive branch) can affect that individual's position on the petit-ideology spectrum. While Idaho, especially since the 1960s, has leaned more to the Jeffersonian side of petit-ideology, having a Wilsonian perspective has been shown to be the most effective approach to governing.

This review of modern Idaho political history shows the value of using petit-ideology as an instrument for political analysis. Examining politics in Idaho through the lens of ideology (i.e., conservative versus liberal) or partisanship (i.e., Democrat versus Republican) simply does not show the true dynamics of the state's political environment. Adding the median position characterized by James Wilson fleshes out the depth of petit-ideology while explaining the most successful activities of the modern-day Idaho governors. While petit-ideology does not answer all questions concerning the motives, beliefs, and actions of all political actors in the state, the approach aids our understanding of some of the principal figures in modern Idaho history. Expanding the use of petit-ideology from historical figures to the institutions of Idaho government seems to be the next logical step.

CHAPTER THREE

The Idaho State Constitution

SHIELD FOR THE WILSONIAN

The constitution of the state of Idaho is quite unremarkable in its content and history.[1] Like most state constitutions, it is long, detailed, and stuck in the nineteenth century. Still, there are aspects of the document peculiar to Idaho that differ significantly from other state constitutions and the U.S. Constitution. Features of the Idaho constitution as they relate to the particular branches and other institutions of the government are discussed in future chapters.[2] This chapter explores some of the eccentricities of the document and how these features have thwarted some of the extremes of petit-ideology.

THE DECLARATION OF RIGHTS: MORE THAN A BILL

Idaho's Declaration of Rights is not buried in amendments tucked away at the end of the constitution. Idaho's founders placed the rights of its citizens prominently in the first article of the document. More numerous than those appended to the U.S. Constitution, Idaho's rights are also more generous. The Declaration of Rights is also at times more detailed and yet more ambiguous than its national counterpart.

The Declaration of Rights begins with allusions to portions of the Declaration of Independence and its vague pronouncement of inalienable rights and the inherent power of people. In a nod to the Civil War the state's constitution makes clear that Idaho is an inseparable part of the Union and that the U.S. Constitution is the supreme law of the land, though Jeffersonians in the state have challenged these notions at times.

The protections granted collectively in the First Amendment to the U.S. Constitution are apportioned to at least three separate sections in the Idaho Declaration of Rights. Freedom of religion is expressed in 150 words and thus with much greater detail, with mention of both free exercise and establishment. Given Idaho's complicated history with the Church of Jesus Christ of Latter-day Saints, much of the fourth section of the Declaration of Rights covers polygamy. While religious freedom is detailed, freedom of speech and press are covered in fewer than 20 words, though citizens are warned that any abuse of these freedoms is their own responsibility. The rights to assemble and petition the government are mirror images of the national norm.

The right to bear arms in the Idaho constitution is much more specific than the Second Amendment of the U.S. Constitution, which results in a clearer delineation of freedoms but also a clearer definition of the limitations to those freedoms. Section 11 of the Declaration of Rights clearly notes how the state has the power to limit the right to keep and bear arms in the areas of concealed carry and by individuals convicted of a felony. The constitutional provision also imposes limits by not allowing the state to require licensure, registration, or special taxation of firearms or the confiscation of such weapons except after the commission of a felony. As with many subjects in the state constitution, more detail is provided than in its federal counterpart.

Two recent amendments have added to the enumerated rights outlined in the Idaho constitution. In 1994 Idaho voters ratified an amendment articulating the rights of crime victims. Victims of crime thus attained legal rights that mirror some of the rights of the accused. These victims' rights were established to counter the expansion of civil liberties of the accused in the criminal justice system. The latest additions of rights listed in the constitution are those to hunt, fish, and trap. Although some voters were uneasy about the right to trap game and some environmentalists thought the amendment would harm habitat, the amendment was overwhelmingly ratified by a vote of the people. The state of Idaho has shown more inclination to adjust rights in its constitution, including marriage (which is not mentioned in the Declaration of Rights), than one sees with the U.S. Constitution. The Declaration of Rights is the most interesting aspect of the tediously long and, in places, confusing state constitution. This examination of the Idaho Declaration of Rights suggests that the Jeffersonian strain of petit-ideology has been evident since the state's founding and has been confirmed with later amendments.

THE LONG AND WINDING CONSTITUTION

Idahoans have included within the state constitution a number of specific policies that could easily have been addressed in legislation. Whether dealing with livestock, water rights, or marriage, it seems contemporary majorities want to make it more difficult for future majorities to alter or jettison current policies. Although scholars studying state constitutions have noted the need for expansive provisions in them due to the unrestricted—except for limitations specified in the U.S. Constitution—and inherent power of state governments, Idahoans seem to want to place many subjects beyond the reach of the state legislature. This makes for a complex text that is referenced by few and understood by even fewer. The body of the state constitution thus reflects much more the Hamiltonian pole of petit-ideology, with its unease about the extremes of democracy.

The Idaho state constitution has extensive articles on subjects that range from water rights, to public and municipal corporations, to public indebtedness and subsidies and even livestock. Like most state constitutions, Idaho's foundational document prescribes in detail much of the minutiae of governance. The U.S. Constitution leaves much to interpretation and has changed through interpretation more often than through amendment. The Idaho constitution lays out in such detail all aspects of government that little is changed through interpretation by the courts and others. As such, amendments—now more than one hundred, a figure likely to increase—are required for often minuscule and technical changes.

The various articles provide details that go beyond what many would believe are appropriate for a constitution. Article III on the state legislature has provisions dealing with the journal for each chamber, the manner by which a bill shall be passed, and how the body and title of a bill should not "embrace" more than one subject. The state legislature is also prohibited from enacting laws of a local or special nature in no fewer than thirty-two enumerated situations. An entire section under the article describing powers of the state legislature explains how gambling is prohibited in the state and gives examples of activities that skirt the prohibition, while another section is devoted to the legislature's power and authority over intoxicating liquors. Almost three hundred words are devoted to compensation of members of the legislature, in contrast to the U.S. Constitution, where Article III, which describes the entire judicial branch of the United States, contains fewer than four hundred words.

The article in the state constitution on the judiciary is no more concise. There are two sections that describe the duties and functions of the clerks of the state supreme court and the district courts. There is a section that provides the definition of treason in a manner similar to the U.S. Constitution, though treason against a state is a peculiar concept. More details are included on the residence of judges and the general procedures for and disposition of cases by the judiciary. Little is left up to interpretation. This intense detail explains why so few cases before the state judiciary in regard to the state constitution are significant or newsworthy, especially in contrast to the rulings of the U.S. Supreme Court.

The detailing of the executive branch, with its own article, follows the same pattern as articles for the other branches. The governor's pardoning power, or lack thereof, takes no fewer than almost 350 words to describe. The governor's veto power requires more than 200 words. To put this in perspective, the pardon power of the president of the United States is a mere clause of a sentence consisting of fewer than 20 words.

Much of the state constitution of Idaho, and of other states, looks more like statutes or laws than a constitution in the manner of the U.S. Constitution. The difference in the length of the documents can be traced to the theoretical differences behind the inherent power of the state versus that of the national government.

The national government was created at a precise time and with a specific action. The ratification of the Constitution was the genesis for the national government. The national government does not have inherent powers in relation to the states and the citizens of the country. Although every sovereign country has inherent powers and the United States is no different, those inherent powers do not extend to the domestic affairs of the nation. The U.S. Constitution grants power to the national government. The prohibitions of certain actions by the government are clarifications to these grants of powers.

The U.S. Constitution is a contract between the national government and the people. Some believe the document is actually between the states and the national government, but that concept should be brushed aside due to the preamble ("We the People") and the arguments by Hamilton. It is a contract based on how John Locke posited the manner by which a society leaves the state of nature. The Constitution therefore is a document that conditionally grants power to the national government. The national government has only the powers the people give to the government. The enumeration of such powers does not have to be expansive, as the national government is one of limited powers.

The states, even those created out of grants of land from the national government, have inherent powers that are available through no action by the public. This concept is articulated in the Tenth Amendment to the Constitution. Although Jeffersonians have used this amendment to expand the power of the states vis-à-vis the national government, it is still a clear indication of the understanding of the state government having vast and extensive plenary powers.

If the state governments have such far-reaching power without the state constitution, then what is the purpose of the state constitution? While the U.S. Constitution grants power, the state government's constitution limits power. It requires more verbiage, articles, and sections in order to describe and delineate prohibitions than it would need to promulgate finite powers. The Idaho state constitution is long because the task of limiting inherent power is so arduous.

Is the Idaho state constitution too long? Probably. Could the document be shortened and made more concise? Most assuredly. This subject has not been completely overlooked by Idahoans, especially government officials. Gov. Robert Smylie suggested in the mid-1960s that a major overhaul of the state constitution be undertaken. He thought that the document should be edited to remove the "cobwebs of bigotry and suspicion and restraint that are not useful to the people in the conduct of this, their government."[3] Similar to the original intention of the constitutional convention of 1787, a commission was created to forward suggestions to the state legislature to consider, and the legislature would then forward proposals to the voters for ratification. Eventually the legislature sent changes to the voters that affected almost two-thirds of the state constitution. Although there was no explicit emphasis on making the document more succinct, the changes were significant. Such radical changes were not palatable to the electorate, however, who voted down the amendments by a clear and significant majority. No subsequent substantial revision has been attempted since. The state constitution of Idaho remains long and winding, though of necessity, in order to restrain the inherent power of the state government.

THE IDAHO CONSTITUTION AS A SHIELD FOR THE WILSONIAN

Government officeholders in Idaho are sworn to uphold the provisions of the state constitution when performing their duties. How this duty is performed is left to the interpretation of the officeholder. Governors in particular can use the state constitution as a shield to protect them from the slings and arrows of Jeffersonians and Hamiltonians and thereby adhere to a Wilsonian position on the petit-ideology arc. Butch Otter is a contemporary example of this phenomenon.

As a Jeffersonian, at least in his youth, Otter was a robust proponent of private ownership and individual freedoms versus government ownership and the curtailment of rights by the majority. The example of privatizing the sale of liquor in the state illuminates how the state constitution can be used to obtain Wilsonian results.

In Idaho retail sales of liquor (not wine or beer) are transacted within a government-controlled system. The state government buys the liquor from producers and sells the bottles to consumers in state-owned liquor stores. This is a clear infringement on the functioning of the free-market system. State control of the distribution of liquor, which exists in some other states as well, is a vestige of the repeal of Prohibition. A true Jeffersonian would decry such a perversion of the free market and demand the government allow private interests to fulfill the desires of the citizens. The problem is that the state-controlled system is quite popular for two reasons: certain religious groups in the state support the government system, including the relatively low number of liquor stores and the limited hours of operation, as a means to discourage the use of alcohol, and the system provides significant revenue to the state government while actually keeping prices low.

Otter has taken a Wilsonian approach that is both pragmatic from a fiscal perspective and politically astute. He has stated that the state liquor delivery system is based on the state constitution's mandate to the legislature for the "promotion of temperance and morality."[4] The constitution states in Article III, section 24, that "the first concern of all good government is the virtue and sobriety of the people, and the purity of the home. The legislature should further all wise and well directed efforts for the promotion of temperance and morality." Such a broad statement could apply to a multitude of situations and does not necessarily call for a state-run liquor distribution system. The state constitution does provide a convenient fig leaf behind which politicians in Idaho can hide their support for a policy that violates their professed beliefs.

Using petit-ideology shows how the document that is the foundation for government in the state of Idaho is a mirror of the political world captured within the state. The state constitution does not grant power to the state government as much as it regulates certain actions and prohibits others. Although it is long and detailed, the document still allows for discretion by government officials to make politically savvy actions that bridge the gap between the Jeffersonians and the Hamiltonians. Metaphorically speaking, a wise person uses a shield to accomplish what a sword cannot.

CHAPTER FOUR

State Legislature

MICROCOSM AND MYSTERY

In structure and operation the Idaho state legislature borrows aspects from both the Jeffersonian and Hamiltonian sides of petit-ideology. Protecting individuals by creating an anemic government with a part-time "citizen" legislature of limited duration and scope is Jeffersonian in nature, while collective decision-making on appropriations by disciplined parties within the legislature, especially in committees, shows the Hamiltonian features of the legislature. The legislature is representative of the state; it is a microcosm of the struggles and compromises played out in the petit-ideology of the broader society. There is also a mystery surrounding the Idaho state legislature. Why are the two chambers viewed as being so different when institutionally they are so similar? The answer is that beliefs are more powerful than institutional structures.

JEFFERSONIAN FEATURES OF THE STATE LEGISLATURE

Jeffersonian values regarding government institutions are reflected in Idaho's legislature. As noted earlier, Jeffersonians perceive the individual as paramount within society and the principal function of government as allowing individuals to pursue their own self-interest and to protect private property. Government in general and the legislature with its power to create laws in particular should, in the Jeffersonian view, be limited in their ability to do harm. For Jeffersonians limits must be placed on the legislative branch so it will not centralize power in the government at the expense of private citizens. The legislature and individual legislators must be kept on a short leash to keep them from preying on citizens.

In order to keep specific legislators from exercising the self-aggrandizement to which Jeffersonians believe they are naturally inclined, legislators must not be given too much freedom or be allowed to act without accountability to the public. Short terms of office followed by having to face the electors from their districts, at least according to democratic theory, keep legislators accountable to their constituents. Anti-Federalists, the earliest Jeffersonians in America, even saw the biennial elections of the U.S. House as too infrequent. The essayist known as "Cato" and others who wrote against the proposed national constitution believed that shorter terms of office would prevent the creation of an aristocracy within government and also allow for the legislature to become, in Cato's words, a nursery of "great and able men."[1]

All members of the Idaho state legislature, both the house and the senate, serve two-year terms. No state legislature in the country has terms of less than two years. Jeffersonians view the short two-year term as a check against legislators losing touch with their constituents and not looking out for the needs of individuals in their district. Even with high reelection rates for incumbents, legislators are seen as less likely to lose sight of the needs of the voters.

Repeated reelection of incumbents has bred attempts to limit the number of terms a legislator may serve. This has been a favored cause of Jeffersonian-leaning citizens since the time of the drafting of the Constitution, when there were calls for mandatory rotation for members of Congress. Currently there are fifteen states that have some form of term limit imposed on their state legislators. Idaho is not among them, but that is not for a lack of initiative from the public.

Idahoans passed an initiative to limit the terms of state legislators in 1994 even though turnover among incumbents was quite high.[2] Turnover and the incumbent-reelection rate were both high, which seems incongruous, since many officeholders left the legislature after serving only a few terms. After trying to override the initiative, the state legislature placed an advisory question on the ballot in 1998. Again the voters signaled their continued, though diminished, support for term limits. One reason suggested for the lower level of support was that this question applied only to state legislators while the first also included members of Congress. Limits on national offices had in the interim been ruled unconstitutional. The state legislature overturned the term-limit initiative in 2002, and a subsequent ballot measure to reinstate the limits came up short that November. The swings back and forth can be seen as a desire of the voters not to move too far from a Wilsonian center.

This common two-year term for both chambers is rare among bicameral legislatures. Only twelve states have the same two-year term for both of their chambers, most of them being in New England. Among western states only Idaho and Arizona have such a structure. This configuration violates a clear principle for limiting power in a legislature by providing each chamber with distinct interests, a topic explored later in this chapter.

Jeffersonians may assume that the state legislature can be restricted in its assault on individual rights and freedoms by limiting the length of its session. The Idaho state legislature originally met only every other year. This situation was not changed until 1968. Biennial sessions, ironically, provided greater power to the governor, who was thus able to have more control over appropriations in the absence of the legislators during times when tax revenues did not match those predicted by two-year budgets.

Although not constitutionally restricted, the state legislature typically meets for only a few months, starting on the second Monday of January each year. The session usually ends at the end of March or beginning of April. The shortest session in recent years was in 2002, when it ended on March 15 after sixty-eight days, while the longest session, in 2003, did not end until May 3 after lasting 188 days. The 2009 session was not adjourned until May 8, but since it had started later in January, it was not as long as the 2003 session. A saying around the state capitol is that the session should not end before St. Patrick's Day or last beyond Easter. Traditionally the session was to end before the farmers serving in the state legislature had to get home to plant their crops.

Fewer legislative days implies fewer chances of passing legislation. Leadership within the state legislature further truncates the ability to pass laws by restricting the introduction of bills after a certain point in the session. Later in the session only committees under the control of leadership (e.g., State Affairs, Ways and Means) may introduce legislation. This process, though Hamiltonian in nature because it restricts the actions of individual legislators, prevents an elongated session and, theoretically, any expansion of the scope of the government.

The abbreviated session creates part-time legislators. Lionized as "citizen" legislators, Idaho's state senators and representatives must have other occupations or other sources of income to compensate for their sub-subsistence-level legislative remuneration. Unlike legislatures that academics identify as "professional," Idaho's falls far below the professional standards of the U.S. Congress in terms of pay, days in session, and professional staff.[3] Individual legislators do not have the assistance of personal staff and must rely on a centralized system of aid—the Legislative Services Office—for help in drafting and researching proposed legislation. This situation would seem to support a Jeffersonian view of individual legislators who are close to their communities and constituents and working without assistance from permanent political operatives. In reality legislators receive assistance from lobbyists who draft bills and may even provide budgetary analysis on proposed legislation. One could see the role of lobbyists as consistent with the Jeffersonian ideal, as they essentially function as an extension of the marketplace. The subject of lobbyists is considered in more depth in chapter 8, which discusses interest groups.

HAMILTONIAN FEATURES OF THE STATE LEGISLATURE

Political parties have been viewed as a means to hold together the disparate facets of a compound republic with separate branches of government. Parties help the process of taking varied and individual interests and aggregating them into policies that are beneficial for the whole of society. According to some scholars, parties "provide the machinery through which members cooperate to make national policy."[4] Parties serve a similar function on the state level. Legislatures with a robust committee system, buttressed by a formal party system such as in Idaho, act as a centripetal force in a very Hamiltonian manner.

Political parties play a significant role in making the state legislature work for a common cause and function less as a body of 105 individuals' interests. Leaders in the Idaho legislature have superior tools for corralling the Jeffersonian instincts of individual representatives and senators. Legislative leaders can direct plum committee assignments to favored members of their own party. While the U.S. Congress has become more democratic in its selection of members and chairs of committees, the party leaders in the Idaho legislature have retained almost complete control over committee assignments. Seniority is *a* factor in the selection of committee chairs, but it is not *the* factor. Recent examples have shown that committee chairs who cross their party's leadership will not keep their positions for long.

Reps. Leon Smith and Tom Trail were removed from their positions as committee chairs by house Speaker Lawerence Denney for not supporting leadership on procedural votes during the 2011 legislative session. Denney noted the reason for their removal as voting too independently. Denney stated at the time, "I don't ask anybody to vote a certain way on any issue, but I do expect them to support other committee chairmen and leadership on procedural issues, and there were several votes this year that they did not support us."[5] Independence from leadership was the principal reason for their ouster. These actions exemplify how party leadership can strengthen the common interest, at least the common interest of a political party.

Such actions by legislative leaders may have unforeseen consequences. During the next postelection organization after Denney stripped Smith and Trail of their committee positions, Republicans in the lower chamber rebuked Denney and chose Scott Bedke as Speaker.[6] Although this move could be thought of on the surface as revenge by the Jeffersonians, it is actually another form of centripetal force at work. Individuals, even the Speaker, cannot act in a manner that is extreme and contrary to the views of the collective, in this case the Republican caucus of the house. The group thus reins in the individual who strays too far afield.

One of the reasons so much attention is paid to committee chairs in the state legislature is the significant power they wield. The chairs have almost complete control over their committees. The agenda of the committee is the domain of the chair. Chairs can kill a bill by "putting it in their drawer." Since chairs control their committees' agenda, they can effectively kill a bill simply by not scheduling a hearing or vote. It is very rare for a chair to be overruled on such an occasion. Respect for the system prevents the use of procedures to overrule chairs' prerogative to support bills or kill them.[7] The influence of the committees, especially of the chairs, enhances the Hamiltonian characteristic of power concentration.

All committees in the Idaho state legislature are influential, but one is supremely powerful. The Joint Finance and Appropriations Committee

(JFAC) is a unique and exceptional feature of the legislature. Made up of members of both the house and the senate, JFAC functions in many respects the way a conference committee does in the U.S. Congress. In Congress a conference committee is usually needed to reconcile differences between similar bills passed by the House and Senate. The difference with JFAC is that the conference is held before either chamber passes a bill.

JFAC is the starting point for spending decisions in the state legislature. Instead of each chamber passing an appropriations bill that has to be reconciled in a conference committee, as is customary in orthodox lawmaking procedures, JFAC holds hearings and approves appropriations bills before any action is taken by the house or the senate. Bills passed by JFAC are usually approved with few or no changes by either chamber.

Many observers view this process as unorthodox if not just plain weird. Upon closer observation, the use of JFAC is rational and logical for an institution that is pressed for time, given the abbreviated session length. Instead of beginning the legislative process within each chamber, the legislature starts with the bicameral stage of the process—finding compromises acceptable to both chambers. A great deal of discretion and respect is shown for the work of JFAC by members of both chambers, thus allowing the entire appropriations side of the budget to be completed quickly, typically in less than three months' time.

The outsized level of control exercised by JFAC is a significant Hamiltonian aspect of the Idaho state legislative process. Leaving the most contentious spending decisions to one body, the legislature speaks with one voice on its paramount mission: setting the budget. The use of JFAC allows for the legislature to focus more precisely on broad goals and objectives, and it is thus less likely to be distracted by the individual and parochial interests within the state.

THE MYSTERY OF BICAMERAL DIFFERENCES

Legislatures are split into separate chambers typically as a means to provide representation to different interests within a society or as a mechanism to curtail the power of the legislature. The goal of diverse representation may be traced to the British need to separate the lords from the commoners in Parliament. Reducing the power of the legislature by dividing and conquering seems related to Montesquieu's *The Spirit of the Laws*, which was the inspiration for the "separation of powers" the U.S. founding fathers included in the Constitution. The Idaho state legislature has two chambers but does not have the institutional differences present in other legislatures.

James Madison provided the clearest and boldest argument for the need for two chambers in a legislature when he wrote his arguments in favor of the U.S. Constitution. A bicameral legislature was one of the "auxiliary precautions" Madison was referring to in *Federalist Paper* No. 51 as necessary for the government to control itself. He saw the Congress as the body that would dominate the government and believed that the remedy for this "inconvenience" was to divide the legislature into different "branches." The simple function of splitting the Congress into two chambers was not a sufficient safeguard, however.

Madison believed that the separate chambers needed to have separate interests. The two bodies needed to be as little connected as possible while still allowing the legislature as a whole to perform its common function of being connected to the people. The most obvious means for ensuring that the two halves of the Congress would have different interests was to require different "modes of election" for each body. How the Senate was chosen as compared to how the House was chosen was not as important as who did the choosing. The House would be elected by the people, while the Senate was chosen by the state legislatures. Although Publius, in *Federalist Paper* No. 62, argues for a senatorial selection process that would provide the states with a means to be involved with the national government (and the public took pride in their own state's individuality), the obvious conflict of interest created by the different selection processes is important for this theoretical argument.[8] Representing different constituents will ensure that there is conflict between the chambers, thus hamstringing the power of the Congress.

The different term lengths for House and Senate members are also seen as a means to serve the public good. The House, with its short two-year terms, would be reflective of changing opinions and positions within society. With the entire House up for election every two years, an ideological or partisan swing in the country would be reflected in the composition of the House almost immediately. The Senate, with its longer six-year terms, would focus more on the long-term interests of the nation. Since only one-third of the Senate at most could change every two years, the

Senate would provide more stability and institutional memory for the Congress while also, according to Publius, leading other countries to have confidence in the government.

When writing about the Senate, Publius provides a more specific argument on the need to represent separate interests. Laws could not be passed without the support of a majority of the people and a majority of the states. Following this principle would not provide an undue advantage for either small or large states and would limit the amount of legislation emanating from Congress, which Publius argued was a positive feature that should be included in the Constitution.

How does the Idaho state legislature differ from the model laid out in the original Constitution? Both the Idaho house and senate are directly elected by the people, and representatives and senators are each elected for two-year terms, which is not uncommon in other states. What is unique is that members of both the house and senate are elected from the same districts. There are thirty-five districts in Idaho, with each district electing one senator and two representatives. As such, the size of the district (i.e., the population) is the same one selecting members for both chambers. The only visible difference is the size of the chambers; the house has twice as many members as the senate. This difference was never considered significant with respect to the national government, and the 2-to-1 ratio is lower than what existed for the Congress in 1789 and of course today as well.

From an institutionalist perspective similar to Madison's, there should be no difference between the interests of the two chambers in the Idaho state legislature. Both sides of the state legislature are selected in the same manner and represent not just the same type of constituents but the same actual constituents. As such, one would expect the two chambers to be very similar in outlook and disposition. However, those who are closest to the legislature do not believe them to be so very alike.

Observers of the Idaho legislature perceive the house to be more conservative than the senate. Interviews with senators who previously have served in the house and journalists who cover both chambers reveal a clear belief in the more conservative bent of the house. This tendency is also noted empirically, through voting records. The Idaho Conservative website rated how often each individual member of the legislature had voted on the conservative side of prominent legislation, thus using an approach similar to the way other interest groups measure the ideological beliefs of Congress members. A review of the ratings for 2007 does not show a large difference overall in conservative voting patterns between the chambers. After taking into account the different percentage of party members in each chamber, since the numbers of Republicans and Democrats vary significantly, the house is more conservative than the senate in this gauge of ideology between the chambers. Currently the Idaho Freedom Foundation creates an index for each state legislator based on how he or she voted on various pieces of legislation. Legislation is given a score according to whether it meets certain criteria determined by the foundation. Although the criteria the group uses to evaluate legislation are based on whether the bill meets libertarian ideals (which would be Jeffersonian ideals in terms of petit-ideology), these measures reflect views that most people would see as conservative. The higher the score, the more often the legislator has voted for bills the foundation deems as supporting freedom, though each bill is not treated equally. For the 2015 legislative session the average score for house members was 3.23, while senators had an average score of 2.39.[9] The averages of these measures reinforce the belief that the house is the more conservative legislative chamber.

So, if there are no significant institutional differences between the senate and house, why are the chambers different? The different size of each chamber may be one of the factors in making the house seem more unruly, less formal, and more emotional than the senate. Size has an effect on differences in rules and committees, according to studies of Congress.[10] Although observers of the Idaho state legislature comment on the effect of size, they see culture and acculturation as more important reasons for the differences between the chambers in Idaho.

Members of the Idaho house and senate view their roles through the prism of the U.S. Congress, at least the Congress as portrayed in simplistic characterizations of the body.[11] The House is for "the people," and the Senate is in theory more "proper" in its decorum. The rules for behavior and dress are more formal in the state senate, while debates are often more heated in the state house. Culture, how one views what it means to be a senator or a representative, influences the actions of the two chambers in the state legislature more than do institutional differences based on term length and constituents. Culture and to some extent size solve the mystery of differences between two chambers that are so similar in structure.

If there are few structural differences between the chambers, should the institutions be altered? It is logical that if the state legislature consists of two chambers that are institutionally very similar, then institutional changes should be considered. As Sen. George Norris of Nebraska stated, "There is no sense or reason in having the same thing done twice, especially if it is to be done by two bodies of men elected in the same way and having the same jurisdiction."[12] Why should Idaho have a bicameral legislature if the tenets of bicameralism are not being followed?

The state of Nebraska tackled this issue early in the twentieth century with an approach that was novel, at least in the United States: get rid of one of the chambers. Nebraska boasts the only state legislature that is unicameral. Nebraska's Senator Norris made the most vocal arguments for changing to a single legislative chamber. Norris believed that, since the United States does not have rigid classes of citizens like the lords and commoners in Britain, there was no need for the state legislature to have two chambers to represent separate interests in society. While others see a bicameral legislature as a protection against centralized power, Norris thought that the conference committees of a bicameral legislature were a corrupting influence. The conference committee, made necessary by having two chambers, is hidden from public view and ripe for coercion by special interest groups. Norris, using stereotypical midwestern common sense, also wondered why a government, whether state or national, needed two bodies to do the same thing. Such duplication was fiscally wasteful in Norris's mind.[13] Norris's advocacy for a unicameral legislative body bore fruit in 1934, when Nebraska voters passed a constitutional amendment to that effect.[14]

To change the Idaho state legislature into a unicameral body would require a similar constitutional amendment. Such a radical change would probably face steep opposition from Idahoans averse to altering the basic structure of the state government, especially to a plan that was dissimilar from the configuration of what most people view as the familiar form of the legislative branch of the U.S. Congress, which was the model for Idaho. A less extreme alteration would seem more practical.

One simple method to differentiate the interests served by each chamber would be to lengthen the term for the senate. Although also requiring a constitutional amendment, extending the term for Idaho senators to four years would differentiate the two bodies but in a familiar manner: that of the U.S. Congress. With a longer term, senators would have a vision of society that was less reflexive and more tempered. Being freed from constant exposure to the whims of the public would allow senators to have more of a Hamiltonian outlook on the state. Splitting the conclusion of the terms for senators would ensure that at most only half of the senate could be changed in one election cycle. Continuity and stability, theoretical hallmarks of the U.S. Senate, would give the Idaho senate an institutional divergence in interests relative to the house.

A proposal to lengthen the terms of state senators was included in the suggested constitutional revision offered by the review commission in the 1960s. Along with changes to the judiciary and the rights of citizens, the change to the senatorial terms was part of a large package to revise and update the state constitution that had been written in haste during the rush to achieve statehood in the nineteenth century. The entire revision was rejected by the voters in 1970, receiving support on less than 35 percent of the ballots cast.[15] Subsequent suggestions for changes to a senator's term of office have not received the necessary support to be placed before the voters for ratification. The belief is that members of the state house think that if they have to run every two years, so should their colleagues in the senate.

A process to have members of the house and senate represent different sets of constituents would not have to clear the hurdle of amending the state constitution. The Idaho state constitution was amended in 1994 to wrest the power of redistricting from the state legislature itself, giving the power to an appointed commission. The constitution limits the number of members in each chamber but does not require that senators and representatives be elected from identical districts. In fact the enacting legislation seems to support creating smaller districts to better represent communities of interest. Idaho Code 72-1506 under "Criteria Governing Plans" notes "to the maximum extent possible, districts shall preserve traditional neighborhoods and local communities of interest." One interpretation of this clause would prohibit redistricting plans that put traditional neighborhoods and communities of interest into large districts where their influence is submerged within the larger community. By having smaller districts for house members (i.e., having each representative elected from a district half the size of a senate district), smaller communities, whether political subdivisions, ethnic or racial minorities, or economic interests, could be represented by one house member, thus better meeting the statutory requirements for districts.

Having the state house consist of seventy members, with each being elected from a separate, distinct, and less populated district, would generate a number of advantages.

Advantages of Change

One advantage of changing the legislature would be that representation of varied interests is enhanced by smaller districts. Smaller districts tend to include a population of citizens with similar views and policy preferences. The representative of this homogeneous constituency can more accurately reflect the views of the constituents when voting on legislation. If the districts cover too much territory, it is difficult for representatives to be in close contact with their constituents. Large districts thus make it difficult for representatives to represent their entire district in the legislature.

Another advantage would be that a candidate who is not well funded but runs a compelling grassroots campaign can have an opportunity to be successful in a smaller district. Local groups can have a greater impact on campaigns in districts that include fewer voters. Smaller districts open up the democratic process to more people.

Large districts dilute the influence of minorities. With a greater number of districts, each with a lower population, the Hispanic community, which is expanding in Idaho but is underrepresented, could have greater influence in the legislature. A similar argument can be made for any minority in the state, whether farmers, ranchers, or Native Americans.

By changing the number of districts through the decennial redistricting process, Idaho could strengthen the bicameral aspects of the state legislature while at the same time improving representation of communities of interest and the electoral process, all without changing the state constitution. A bicameral legislature whose two chambers are perceived to be different only through custom and size could have an institutionalized enhancement to provide the potential benefits of having both a house and a senate. Why the two chambers are different would be less of a mystery and would instead be more embedded in the institutional fabric of the legislature.

Petit-ideology provides a clear means to gain an understanding of the institution of the Idaho state legislature. The institution includes aspects of both the Jeffersonian and Hamiltonian systems of belief regarding the government and the individual. As with the state overall, the legislature is a combination of both ends of the petit-ideology spectrum. No measure seems to clearly decipher the lack of bicameral differences in the legislature. With two chambers so similar, is there a need for both?

CHAPTER FIVE

Idaho's Governor

HAMILTONIAN IN A JEFFERSONIAN EXECUTIVE BRANCH

By the nature of the position, a governor is seen as the leader of state government. The governor, like the president, is often portrayed as a heroic figure who rises above the pettiness of party and leads the legislature to enact policies in the best interest of the entire community. Such a political figure assumes all of the hallmarks of the Hamiltonian side of petit-ideology. The executive branch in Idaho, however, is composed of eight separately elected officials, each of whom is head of his or her own fiefdom. Dividing up the power of the executive branch is in the truest sense a Jeffersonian means of circumscribing the power of government, especially the most potentially tyrannical branch. In Idaho the Hamiltonian governor thus serves in a Jeffersonian executive branch.

THE HAMILTONIAN GOVERNOR: FORMAL POWERS

The term "Hamiltonian," coined by James MacGregor Burns to represent a model of leadership for the president of the United States, is basically the same as the term "Hamiltonian" in the petit-ideology sense. In Burns's Hamiltonian model of presidential leadership the president is heroic and above partisan politics and party intrigue, and the president should lead in all policy areas. Congress should follow the president's lead in policy, but if they don't the president should proceed without Congress. The Hamiltonian model of the presidency has the government revolve around the president, who exhibits "energy, resourcefulness, inventiveness, and ruthless pragmatism."[1] This model is true to the vision of government as illustrated in the Hamiltonian approach of petit-ideology. These qualities for a president can easily be transferred to a governor.

Governors, regardless of their formal powers, often follow the Hamiltonian model. As a single executive, the governor is the only figure in state government who can lead with a single voice. This view was touted by Hamilton when arguing for the Constitution in the *Federalist Papers*, where he often compared the president to the powerful governor of New York. Idahoans have traditionally seen their governors as providing the leadership role for the state government.

Governors are often characterized as strong or weak based on the powers allotted to them in the state constitution. Joseph Schlesinger created an "Index of Formal Powers" for the governors of each state. A common menu of formal gubernatorial powers includes the powers of tenure, appointment, budget, organization, and veto. A review of these powers shows that Idaho's governor has sufficient powers to serve in a Hamiltonian style. According to Schlesinger's formula, the formal powers of the governor of Idaho were considered close to the median in 1965, strong in 1983, and moderate in 2003.[2] The lower values in the earlier studies were due to the weak budgeting power, which has since been strengthened. The formal powers of the Idaho governor, as examined below, provide sufficient resources for the officeholder to follow the Hamiltonian model of leadership.

Tenure of office is measured by two criteria: the length of term and the ability to serve consecutive terms. Idaho since 1946 elects its governors for four-year terms, and since 1956 governors have been able to serve consecutive terms. Idahoans have rewarded many of their governors with multiple terms, allowing the executive to wield substantial power and have the latitude to cement their programs firmly into the state. Since Robert Smylie was first given the opportunity to serve a four-year term as governor and to serve more than one term, Idaho governors have served for extended periods. Smylie was elected three times and served twelve years; Cecil Andrus was elected four times and served fourteen years, resigning in his second term to serve as U.S. secretary of the interior; John Evans was elected two times and served ten years, including two years of Andrus's second term; Butch Otter has been elected three times and will complete twelve years in 2019. Only two recent governors have been elected to a single term: Don Samuelson, who lost his reelection bid, and Phil Batt, who chose not to run for a second term. The possibility of long tenures for Idaho's governors supports a strong office.

Some governors view their appointment power as "the most important weapon in their arsenal when it comes to managing the state bureaucracy."[3] The ability to shape an administration through the appointment of personnel is essential for effective governance. Governors do not have as much discretion as presidents, since some of the other principal offices of state executive branches are elected separately. Many lower positions in the executive branch are appointed at the discretion of boards and commissions; however, in Idaho the governor appoints the members of those boards and commissions. Still, Idaho governors have more power when it comes to appointments outside the executive branch, which allows them to influence other branches and levels of state government.

When a vacancy exists in the state legislature or judiciary in Idaho, the governor is endowed with the power to fill the open position. Some see the power to fill vacancies in the executive branch as patronage that can be used in the governor's battle with the legislative branch.[4] However, being able to appoint members of the legislature seems even more advantageous. When a vacancy occurs in the Idaho state legislature, according to Idaho Statutes Title 59, the governor picks a replacement from among three nominees chosen by the legislative district committee of the political party of the former member whose seat is vacant. The nominating function of the local party circumscribes the governor's discretion to an extent but still gives the governor the ability to shape the legislature, even if only on the margins. Some governors have spurred the process by appointing a member of the legislature to an executive position and then choosing the new appointee's replacement. Vacancies in the judiciary are filled solely at the governor's discretion, as the judges and justices are elected in nonpartisan elections, thus eliminating the nominating role for the local political parties.

Governors in Idaho also have a role in appointing officials to other levels of government. For openings on county commissions, a process similar to that used for state legislators is followed, the only difference being the appropriate county instead of district party committee submits nominations to the governor. Vacancies in city governments are ordinarily filled by the mayor and city council, but in extraordinary circumstances, such as when there is not a quorum of the city council to make an appointment, the governor can fill the necessary positions on the city councils.[5] Governors in Idaho, as in most states, make appointments to the U.S. Senate when vacancies occur. Seven times Idaho governors have chosen replacements to serve the remainder of a Senate term. Being able to shape the makeup of other branches of the state government and other levels of government in the federal system enhances the ability of the governor to have influence on the state executive branch and beyond.

Gubernatorial control over the budget is more significant than it may first appear. In Idaho the governor presents a budget to the legislature just days after the beginning of their session. In the past Idaho governors, besides giving a state of the state address, would present a separate budget address to the legislature. In recent years the two presentations have been combined. The power to appropriate funds and enact taxes is clearly a power of the state legislature, but the ability to set the agenda, as the governor does for the budget and other issues, should not be underestimated.

Studies have measured the influence of presidents on the agenda of Congress. These findings likely also would apply to governors and state legislatures. If anything, in Idaho the governor should be able to sway the policies under consideration more than a U.S. president can. Members of the Idaho state legislature have very limited resources to perform research on proposals. Without personal assistants and with limited institutional staff, individual members of the legislature are often at the mercy of the governor and lobbyists—discussed later—to decide not just how to vote on proposed legislation but also what issues should be the subject for discussion and consideration.

Governors have an impact not only on issues placed on the agenda of the legislature but also on issues that are kept off the agenda. As developed by Peter Bachrach and Morton Baratz, non-decision-making—the ability to preclude issues from appearing on the agenda—may be more effective in controlling the arc of policy creation than the power to place topics on the agenda. Non-decision-making is when "status quo oriented persons and groups influence those community values and those political institutions which tend to limit the scope of actual decision-making to 'safe' issues."[6] If the governor omits an item from the budget, the state legislature is less likely to take up the issue.

In 2012 Governor Otter proposed that the state legislature set up a state-run health insurance exchange.[7] Although the state legislature initially rejected the exchange in 2012, they reversed themselves the following year. What changed? In his 2013 State of the State and Budget Address, the governor proposed a state-based health insurance exchange and rejected the proposal to expand Medicaid.[8] By taking Medicaid off the agenda, the governor improved his chances of getting the legislature to approve the exchange. Control of what goes on the agenda—and conversely what does not—is an effective formal power of the governor.

The organizational power of the governor is considered moderate, as the officeholder does not have the ability to reorganize the executive branch without consent from the legislature. The governor also shares the executive branch with seven other elected officers. In contrast, the governor does have the power to appoint a large number of positions.[9] The state constitution even limits the number of departments and seeks to restrain any additional powers being assigned to those departments. This provision seems to place a Jeffersonian constraint on the Hamiltonian governor. As no recent governor has attempted a major reorganization of state government, the organizational power of the Idaho governor is more potential than actual.

The governor's veto power is similar to the power given to the president, yet in many ways the Idaho governor's power is more extensive and forceful. The Idaho executive wields a line-item veto for appropriation bills and has many more opportunities to employ an absolute "pocket" veto.

As in most states, Idaho's governor has the ability to veto specific items from appropriation bills without vetoing the entire spending measure. This line-item veto power provides the governor with immense influence on the budget. The line-item veto is typically thought of as a means for the governor to eliminate profligate spending by the legislature, yet Gov. Dirk Kempthorne in 2003 vetoed budget-cutting measures passed by the state legislature in order to force subsequent passage of an increase to the sales tax he supported.[10]

Like the president of the United States, the governor of Idaho can exercise a "pocket" veto. If the legislature has adjourned sine die, the governor is not able to return a bill passed by the legislature and thus the bill "dies" without being formally vetoed by the governor. This circumstance is more prevalent with the Idaho legislature than with Congress; it happens after each annual session, which is typically characterized by a flurry of legislation immediately before adjournment. The slight difference with the Idaho pocket veto is that the governor must still file any objections to the bill with the Idaho secretary of state within ten days (Sunday excepted) or the bill will become law.

The use of the veto is not a sign of strength by the governor but can be seen as an indication of weakness. As with the other visible formal powers of the office, its use shows an inability to convince the legislature or other portions of government to acquiesce to the governor's will.

Two more formal powers, though not often delineated by others, can prove effective for an Idaho governor. The power of reprieve and pardon for the Idaho governor is circumscribed and joint in operation. The governor alone cannot grant a reprieve or pardon; that power ultimately lies with the Pardons and Parole Board. The board is the only entity that can take positive action, but the governor is provided with the power to reject decisions by the board. In essence the governor cannot grant a pardon but can prevent a pardon.

Maybe the most dramatic case in recent history involved the convicted murderer Donald Paradis, who was on death row for the killing of a woman in Idaho. The Pardons and Parole Board commuted Paradis's sentence from death to life in prison due to doubts concerning Paradis's role in the murder. Gov. Phil Batt had to consider whether to sustain the decision of the board or return Paradis to death row. Batt finally determined that there was substantial doubt. Later another prisoner pleaded guilty to the murder. Batt concluded, "I'm glad I didn't order his execution."[11] The Idaho constitution gives the Hamiltonian governor only an annulling power with respect to criminal justice penalties.

According to the state constitution, Idaho governors have the usual power to call the state legislature into "extra" session on "extraordinary occasions." This power is broader than what the president has, since the governor can prescribe, through the proclamation calling the special session, the specific subjects the state legislature can address. Likewise the governor is under no obligation at any time to call for a special session, and the legislature cannot call itself into a special session.[12] Governors have had mixed success with calling the state legislature into special session.

The state legislature met in special session for a single day in 2000 to make a legislative fix for electric utilities after a federal appeals court ruling on deregulation of the industry. Most other special sessions of the recent past have also dealt with minor issues and were not very substantive.[13] The exception was in 1965.

After the U.S. Supreme Court's ruling in *Reynolds v. Sims* (1964), state legislatures had to be reapportioned to meet the requirement of "one person, one vote." Idaho's state senate was egregiously out of compliance, as there were forty-four senators, one per county regardless of population. In 1965 Governor Smylie called the legislature into extraordinary session on the day immediately following the adjournment of the regular session. The special session, wrestling with only this one subject (reapportionment), took six days to come up with a solution, though they also had to make changes to the congressional and state house districts, which did not take long. The legislature concocted a plan that created multicounty districts that would nominate one senator from each party from each county. This convoluted plan was an attempt to keep the current system in place while pretending to abide by the high court's ruling, even though the legislators knew they were out of compliance.[14] The problem with redistricting and reapportionment would not be completely settled for more than twenty years and then only after a change to the state constitution and a short flirtation with the temporarily attractive concept of floterial districts.

In August 2006 Jim Risch, who ascended to the governorship when Dirk Kempthorne was appointed secretary of the Department of the Interior by Pres. George W. Bush, called an "extraordinary" session of the state legislature that lasted all of one day. With the skyrocketing values of homes due to the housing bubble, property taxes were increasing rapidly. The one piece of legislation that passed during the session moved the responsibility for funding school maintenance and operations from the local property tax and shifted it to the state. In turn the state sales tax was increased from 5 percent to 6 percent to provide funding for the state to meet its obligations.[15] Since it was an election year, a movement to cut property taxes was popular and the short-term governor could bring it to fruition. As home values plummeted during the Great Recession, state funding for schools dropped dramatically, causing spending cutbacks and the need for subsequent local school district levies.

THE HAMILTONIAN GOVERNOR: INFORMAL POWERS

Many writers have expended a great deal of ink remarking on the various informal powers at the disposal of a governor. A review of this hair-splitting effort to itemize different powers makes it clear that there is really only one informal power: the power to persuade.[16] As described and defined by Richard Neustadt in his book *Presidential Power and the Modern Presidents*, the power to persuade is one that also belongs to governors and that encompasses the specific informal powers described by others.

The power to persuade is essentially the capacity to get people to do the governor's bidding while making them believe they ought to do it for their own sake and on their own authority. This power is not based simply on charm but flows from status and authority. The aforementioned formal powers are enhanced and embellished by the power to persuade. Neustadt identified this potential asset for a president to overcome the "separate institutions sharing power" of the national government, but it can easily be transformed into the means for a governor to be successful in overcoming centrifugal forces at the state level.[17]

The power to persuade is similar to bargaining when the executive is interacting with the legislature.[18] Governor Smylie used the power to persuade brilliantly when in 1955 he convinced the state legislature to pass a constitutional amendment to allow him to run for additional terms as governor. As that year's legislative session was winding down, there were three "gridlocked issues" holding up adjournment: reopening Lewis-Clark State College, a bond issue for a new library at the University of Idaho, and the succession bill. Although making no quid pro quo agreements, Smylie made it clear to the supporters of Lewis-Clark State, including the powerful Democratic boss Tom Boise, that "it would be much easier to approve" the college bill, which was sitting on the governor's desk, if the other two bills passed the legislature.[19] With the formal power of the veto behind him, Smylie used persuasion to convince the legislature and Boise to push for passage of the succession bill. No threats were brandished nor was explicit horse trading involved to convince the other participants that they should do what the governor wanted, as it was in their own best interest.

Idaho governors, at least the most successful of them, have used persuasion in many of their interactions with assorted political players. Two of the more cogent examples both deal with the national government and nuclear waste: Cecil Andrus's use of the state police to block shipments of nuclear waste to Idaho and Phil Batt's nuclear waste agreement.

Andrus during his many years as governor had fought the federal government over shipments of nuclear waste to Eastern Idaho. Problems came to a head in 1988, when Andrus decided to block the shipment of material from the Rocky Flats nuclear weapons plant in Colorado. Using the visually appealing media image of a brawny Idaho state trooper standing with his arms crossed and blocking the railroad tracks, Andrus was able to persuade the Department of Energy to negotiate with the state on nuclear waste.[20]

Phil Batt succeeded Andrus as governor and used similar tactics, not only with the federal government but also with the public. Batt negotiated an agreement with the Department of Energy that would limit future nuclear waste shipments and require the removal of nuclear waste from Idaho. Even though Andrus did not agree with all aspects of Batt's pact, he did not support a referendum to revoke the deal.[21] Besides needing to get what he felt was the best deal possible from the federal government, Batt also had to persuade the public of the virtue of the agreement. Governor Batt, through formal debates and a personal appeal, was able to persuade the voting public, despite media-savvy pleas by opponents of the deal, to reject the referendum as not in the best interests of the people of Idaho.[22] The power to persuade, when used with the more formal powers of the office, allows the governor to accomplish many policy goals in dealings with various political actors and to provide leadership in the manner that Hamilton saw as essential for a chief executive.

THE JEFFERSONIAN EXECUTIVE BRANCH

The president in the national government is a singular, almost monarchical figure. No person can serve in any prominent position in the executive branch without being nominated by the president. Most serve at the pleasure of the president. The ability to install loyal colleagues and banish insolent adversaries has, since the time of Andrew Jackson, allowed presidents to single-handedly rule over the executive functions of the national government. This power allows a president to function as a leader in the manner that Hamilton thought most advantageous.

Governors do not have such luxuries. On average, states elect nine executive branch officers separately from the governor. Those who share executive powers with the governor and are elected separately are not indebted to the governor for their position. A Jeffersonian principle that "minimum power should be shared by the maximum number of people" has been espoused in different contexts and for different government structures.[23] Constitutions of the states have disseminated power to many positions, thus making the state executive branch more Jeffersonian in character.

Idaho currently elects six executive branch officials in addition to the governor: lieutenant governor, secretary of state, state controller, state treasurer, attorney general, and superintendent of public instruction. Most of these positions are principally administrative in nature and do not wield much power. Generally the secretary of state runs elections and keeps records for the state, the state controller is the financial record keeper, and the state treasurer invests the funds of the state government. The other three positions are often more interesting.

The attorney general is the chief legal counsel for the state and defends the state if statutes are challenged. This position is sometimes hamstrung, while at other times it provides the officeholder a great deal of discretion. While serving as attorney general, Lawrence Wasden sued the Idaho Department of Lands for actions taken by the State Land Board of Commissioners even though the attorney general is a member of the latter. In this instance, Wasden was in the minority on the board's vote. The board was forced to hire outside attorneys since the attorney general had brought the suit and thus could not defend the board. At the same time, Wasden was suing the federal government on behalf of the governor and others in connection with the Affordable Care Act.[24] The independence of the position by virtue of direct election allows the attorney general to act contrary to the governor and other members of the executive branch.

The state superintendent of public instruction has limited administrative power but often exerts influence as the principal spokesperson for education in the state. The superintendent presents to the state legislature an education budget that is often in conflict with the budget offered by the governor. The superintendent runs the Department of Education but must share power and responsibility with the state's Board of Education, though the superintendent is a member of the board. Those who have held the position in recent years have advocated for education policies based on their own prerogative. Tom Luna proposed a series of significant policy changes in the wake of his 2010 reelection as superintendent. Subsequently known as the Luna Laws, the proposals obtained support from the governor and state legislature. A coalition of groups, including many educators, successfully placed a referendum on the ballot and won repeal of Luna's changes just two years after he had been reelected.[25] Superintendents of public instruction are only as powerful as their persuasive powers over the governor, the state legislature, and, obviously, the people.

The lieutenant governor's role is patterned after that of the vice president of the United States yet, in words attributed to Vice President John Nance Garner, might not be preferable to a bucket of warm spit. Like the vice president, the lieutenant governor presides over the senate and assumes the governorship in case the governor cannot perform the duties of the office. As president of the senate, the lieutenant governor physically presides much more often than the vice president, and there have been individuals in the position who have wielded some influence over the body. In recent times both John Evans and Jim Risch have assumed the governor's office when the sitting governor, Andrus and Kempthorne, respectively, were appointed secretary of the interior. Only Evans went on to run for governor and serve his own term. The post has otherwise not been a stepping stone to the governor's office, though Phil Batt and Butch Otter became governor after a period of time subsequent to serving as lieutenant governor. Where the lieutenant governor in Idaho is significantly different than the vice president is when the governor is absent from the state.

If the governor leaves the state of Idaho for whatever reason, the lieutenant governor, according to the state constitution, assumes the "powers, duties, and emoluments of the office" for the duration of the absence. This situation has revealed the potential for power if not mischief by the lieutenant governor, especially when the governor and lieutenant governor are of different parties.

In 1962 Sen. Henry Dworshak died in office. As governor, Robert Smylie, a Republican, was empowered to appoint a replacement. The lieutenant governor was William Drevlow, a Democrat. An issue developed when Smylie was considering whether to attend Dworshak's funeral, which was to be held in Washington D C. Drevlow related to Smylie that Democrats were pressuring him as lieutenant governor to appoint someone from their party when Smylie was out of town. Given the situation, Smylie chose not to attend the funeral even though Dworshak had served Idaho in Congress for more than twenty years.[26]

In 1987, only a month after being sworn in as lieutenant governor, Butch Otter assumed the governor's chair temporarily while Governor Andrus was out of the state. Congress had passed a bill that would withhold highway funding from any state that did not raise its drinking age to twenty-one. In order to keep the money flowing into the state, the state legislature passed a bill changing the state's legal age from nineteen to twenty-one. Otter, who at the time was firmly on the Jeffersonian end of petit-ideology, vetoed the bill because he thought it meant succumbing to blackmail by the federal government. Although Andrus would return to the state to sign another bill adjusting the drinking age, Otter had shown the independence and, though temporary, the power of the lieutenant governor in Idaho's executive branch.[27]

With a divided executive branch, all governors of Idaho, if they are to succeed, have to rely on their informal power to persuade even more so than do presidents. Only a governor who follows the model of leadership prescribed by Hamilton can overcome the institutional barriers to power erected within the Jeffersonian executive branch.

Much like the legislative branch in Idaho, the executive branch blends aspects of both the Jeffersonian and Hamiltonian sides of petit-ideology. The executive in any government naturally leans to the Hamiltonian end of the spectrum. The executive, or at least a governor, is the single embodiment of the state as a whole. The governor would naturally lean toward favoring the community rather than the individual. Jeffersonians would see this as a potentially abusive aspect of the government. To counter the centripetal force of the governor, the Idaho government provides for other executive officers who are elected separately and thus at least electorally independent of the governor. This multiple-executive branch structure provides the Jeffersonian counterbalance to the Hamiltonian governor. As in the rest of Idaho government, neither position is exclusive and a melding of the two form a balance for the state.

CHAPTER SIX

The State Judiciary

IDAHO'S SAPLESS BRANCH

Alexander Hamilton, in *Federalist Paper* No. 78, contends that the judiciary, due to "the nature of its functions," will be the least likely to intrude upon the political rights of the citizens of the country or the other branches of the government. While the legislature has the power of the purse and creates laws that regulate the actions of citizens and while the executive has the power of the sword and the ability to dispense honors, the feeble judiciary, according to Hamilton, has only judgment and must rely on the other branches to enforce its judgments.

History has shown that Hamilton's description of the scrawny judiciary branch having sand kicked in its face by the big bad Congress and president is largely fallacious. The Supreme Court of the United States, from its rulings in *Marbury v. Madison*, to *Dred Scott*, to *Plessy v. Ferguson*, to *Lockner*, to *Kurematsu*, to *Brown*, to *Roe v. Wade*, to *Citizens United*, has shown that it is more than a match for the other branches in having an effect on the rights of citizens of the nation.

Why was Hamilton wrong? Did Hamilton write what he sincerely believed to be true, with only time and circumstances proving him wrong? Or did Hamilton understand the potential for the courts but downplay that potential influence so as to not frighten those skeptical of the new national government under the Constitution? What is more important is that there are strains of Hamilton's characterization of the judiciary that survive to this day.

Idaho's state judiciary seems to fit Hamilton's description more aptly. Historically the state courts in Idaho seldom issue opinions or verdicts that significantly expand or circumscribe the rights of citizens of the state. Is the court system inherently weak or has an ideology of judicial restraint affected the actions of the courts? The structure of the courts and the culture that underlies that structure may be the source of the lack of influence by the state courts. The unified court system of Idaho is a concentrated organization that fits into a Hamiltonian view of government. Again, like the other branches of the state government, the judiciary includes aspects of both Jeffersonian and Hamiltonian petit-ideology.

THE STRUCTURE OF THE IDAHO COURT SYSTEM

The original structure of the Idaho court system was created by the state constitution and consisted of a supreme court and general common pleas courts. After a major reform of the system in the 1960s and 1970s and the creation of the appeals court in 1981, Idaho's courts included semblances of the four types of courts found in most other states: trial courts of limited jurisdiction, trial courts of general jurisdiction, intermediate appellate courts, and the court of last resort or supreme court. Idaho's court system is a unified system, meaning all lower courts are supervised and administered by the state supreme court. The trial-level courts are divided into eight districts throughout the state.[1]

Trial Courts of Limited Jurisdiction

Until 1971 Idaho had a hodgepodge of courts that performed the functions of a typical court of limited jurisdiction.[2] Newly formed magistrate courts (actually divisions of the district courts mentioned later) took over the functions of the probate, justice, and municipal courts.[3]

The Magistrate Division of the District Court houses the limited jurisdiction courts in Idaho. Magistrates handle six types of proceedings:

- Misdemeanors
- Civil matters involving amounts up to $10,000
- Preliminary hearings (on whether to bind a defendant over for trial on a felony charge)
- Probate cases (wills and estates)
- Juvenile cases (including neglect)
- Domestic relations (divorce, alimony, support, and custody)

Rulings by magistrates are heard on appeal by district judges.

The Magistrate Division also provides for what is sometimes called the "People's Court" or Small Claims Department. Small claims cannot exceed $4,000 in value, and the actions are heard without attorneys or juries. Rulings of these courts may be appealed to another magistrate.

There are eighty-seven magistrate positions authorized in the state of Idaho. Magistrates do not need to have law degrees to serve; a high school diploma or its equivalent is sufficient. When there is a vacancy, magistrates are initially appointed by a magistrate commission made up of county commissioners and other officials in the judicial district where the opening exists. The initial appointment lasts up to eighteen months, when, if the commission feels the magistrate's performance has been satisfactory, the probationary period ends. The magistrate then may stand in a retention election for a four-year term. Subsequent retention elections are required at the end of each term. Involuntary removal from office is handled by the Idaho Judicial Council.

The Idaho Judicial Council

Before the discussion of other levels and manners of courts in the Idaho system, an examination of the judicial council for the state is in order. The Idaho Judicial Council is an arm of the state supreme court and assists the court in maintaining the constitutionally required unified system.

The Judicial Council was created by legislation in 1967 as part of a flurry of state judicial reforms during a period that included the creation of the seven judicial districts.[4] The council is made up of seven members: three attorneys appointed by the state bar's board of commissioners, three non-attorneys appointed by the governor, and the chief justice of the state supreme court. All appointed members must be confirmed by the state senate.

The council acts as a body in the area of the appointment of new justices and judges and the removal of sitting justices and judges. In the event of a vacancy on the state supreme court, state appellate court, or one of the district courts, the council recommends appointments to the governor. The council can recommend between two and four persons for a vacancy, and the governor must choose one of those nominees. The council is also responsible for the discipline and, if needed, removal of sitting justices and judges. The council investigates potential grounds for removal and passes its recommendations on to the state supreme court, which makes the final decision. This procedure illustrates the unified structure of the state court system.

Trial Courts of General Jurisdiction

The courts of general jurisdiction for the state are the courts in each of the seven judicial districts staffed by district judges. Created in the 1960s, the district courts of the state handle the most substantial cases, both criminal and civil, at the trial stage. In general the district courts have jurisdiction over the following types of cases:

- Felonies
- Civil cases without regard to dollar limit (usually personal injury)
- Domestic relations (though these are usually left to magistrates)
- Postconviction relief (defendant challenging a conviction or sentence)
- Appeals from magistrate courts
- Appeals from state agencies and boards

Thirty-seven district judge positions are authorized over the seven judicial districts. Vacancies are filled by the Idaho Judicial Council and the governor, as noted above. District judges serve four-year terms and are elected in nonpartisan elections. In recent years more judges and justices are running against opponents, often well-financed ones. This is a shift from the historical pattern, in which jurists, after attaining office, usually ran unopposed.

Intermediate Appellate Court and Court of Last Resort

Idaho's court of appeals was not created until the state was almost one hundred years old. Although this intermediate appellate court has a similar name to its federal counterpart, Idaho's unified court system makes the appeals court truly an instrument of the state supreme court.

Idaho's supreme court during the 1970s was overwhelmed with the appellate workload of the system. While various alternatives were proposed, including increasing the number of justices on the state supreme court, the legislature finally passed legislation to create the intermediate appellate court, which began operation at the beginning of 1982.[5]

The difference between the federal court system and the Idaho court system centers on the initial handling of appeals. In Idaho, if attorneys appeal a case from the district court, the appeal goes directly to the state supreme court. The justices of the state supreme court then decide whether they will hear the appeal directly or whether the appeal will be turned over to the appeals court. The state supreme court, due to the unified structure of the system, decides not only which cases it will hear but which cases the appeals court will hear. Usually the cases considered the most important or controversial are heard by the supreme court without a hearing before the intermediate court. More routine cases are first argued at the appeals court level. A claimant may appeal a decision of the appeals court to the supreme court, but the higher court decides whether to hear the case or not, again giving the supreme court of the state control over how cases are handled within the state court system.

Justices of Idaho appellate courts, according to the state constitution, run in nonpartisan elections for six-year terms. Although elections to the state supreme court were hotly contested affairs in the early years of the state, there were no contested elections of seats on the supreme court from 1970 until 1994. During this time, with regard to the state supreme court and to a lesser extent the appeals court, Idaho was operating as a de facto Missouri Plan state.

The Missouri Plan, in its purest form, eliminates judicial elections in which candidates compete against each other. When a judicial vacancy occurs in any of the more than twenty states that use this merit-based plan, a judicial nominating commission will recommend names of prospective justices to the governor. The governor must appoint one of the commission's nominees to the vacant post. A retention election is then held a few years later, with voters given the choice only of whether to retain the justice or not.

In Idaho a tradition had developed where justices would step down from the court before their term was over, thus allowing the governor to appoint their replacement after receiving nominations from the Judicial Council. The current justice would then not be challenged in a competitive election, making Idaho voters even less involved in selecting the state's highest jurists than voters in most other states.

Tradition began to fade in the 1990s. First, the tradition of not challenging a sitting justice was overturned in 1994, when Wayne Kidwell ran against Justice Cathy Silak, though she retained her seat at that point. Silak faced a challenger again in 2000 and lost her seat to Daniel Eismann in a race that saw partisan tentacles creeping into a nonpartisan election. Justice Byron Johnson toppled the other pillar of judicial tradition by serving out his term, which triggered a spirited race that had to be settled in a runoff. Kidwell, who was elected to succeed Johnson, also retired at the end of his term, though only one candidate, Jim Jones, ran for the seat. The turn of the twenty-first century has seen more contested judicial elections, though incumbent justices rarely lose their seats.

The campaigns for judicial office in Idaho have recently included not only competition but well-financed competition. The 1990s saw a significant increase in the amounts spent by candidates, while in 2002 an outside group spent more than $170,000 to unseat a justice.[6] Although elections are often seen as providing a measure of public accountability to the courts, campaigns for seats on courts are not immune to the same issues that influence elections at all levels.

MIXED STRUCTURE AND CULTURE

When looking at the structure of the judiciary in Idaho, one finds aspects of both Hamiltonian and Jeffersonian petit-ideology. How citizens and those involved in the judiciary act—what one might label the culture of the judiciary—also shows a conflict between the essences of both sides of petit-ideology.

The state constitution in Article V, section 2, mandates the unified and integrated nature of the Idaho judicial branch: "The courts shall constitute a unified and integrated judicial system for administration and supervision by the Supreme Court." In this capacity the state supreme court is the supervisor and administrator of the entire state court system. It is the purview of the state supreme court to establish statewide rules and policies for the operation of its own functions as well as those of the other courts in the system, including the district courts. As noted earlier, supervision by the state supreme court extends to determining which cases it will hear on appeal directly and which cases will be appealed to the state appeals court before the state supreme court, or if the case will eventually be heard by the state's high court.

This aspect of Idaho's judicial system aligns more closely with the centralized and hierarchical petit-ideology of Hamilton. Those who are the most experienced and qualified, as measured by their attainment of the highest offices, are to direct and command the lower rungs of the judicial ladder. This unified structure also creates a centripetal force that makes the judicial branch more focused on itself and less influenced by democratic forces.

Still, the writers of the state constitution must have believed, as Hamilton did when expressing his views in *Federalist Paper* No. 78, that the judiciary would be the weakest branch of the government and would constantly have to defend itself against the other branches, especially the state legislature. Thus, Article V, section 13, of the Idaho constitution prevents the state legislature from infringing on the jurisdiction of the courts: "The legislature shall have no power to deprive the judicial department of any power or jurisdiction which rightly pertains to it as a coordinate department of the government." The legislature is limited to determining the structure of the courts below the supreme court, similar to the power given to Congress in the U.S. Constitution, and to prescribing mandatory minimum sentences. Whether Hamilton himself actually believed the judiciary needed protection or not, the authors of the Idaho constitution seemed to agree with this logic.

At a more basic level the structure of the court system has clear ties to Jeffersonian principles. While Hamilton, in *Federalist Paper* No. 78, made a spirited argument in favor of justices being appointed to serve for as long as they engage in "good behavior," often conceived as a lifetime term, Idaho judges and justices are elected by the public at large for fixed terms. The magistrates are first appointed but must then go before the public in retention elections. Having the public in such control of the selection of judges and justices fits into the Jeffersonian belief in the virtue of the people and their right to decide who will serve them in government.

Judicial elections in Idaho have changed over the years. Initially judiciary elections in the state were partisan affairs, with justices running as Democrats or Republicans. Beginning in 1934 all candidates ran without party labels, a practice that continues to this day.[7] It is hard to tell whether Hamilton or Jefferson would have preferred partisan elections of judges. Both reflected the late eighteenth-century aversion to political parties, though both also were two of the most fervent party activists in the early years of the nineteenth century. Still, the direct election of judges and justices is inconsistent with the unified judicial structure of the state of Idaho.

Institutions and government structure have only a partial effect on behavior and actions. The beliefs of participants in the system also affect the how members of the government act. Participants include both office-holders and the public at large. As seen with the structure of the judiciary, the culture surrounding the state court system is also divided between aspects of Hamiltonian and Jeffersonian petit-ideology.

The Idaho courts have traditionally not played a significant role in forming public policy for the state. While other states saw courts as being engines for social change after the end of Earl Warren's service as chief justice of the U.S. Supreme Court in the late 1960s, when the court delved into areas of segregation, rights of criminal defendants, reapportionment, and the First Amendment, Idaho courts were considered more "centrist" or "conservative."[8] A detailed evaluation of major rulings of the state supreme court during the 1980s concluded that it "refrained from participating in making public policy." The courts (at least during the 1980s) looked to the state legislature to rectify anomalies or unfairness in Idaho laws. The courts were also hesitant to disturb common law doctrines of earlier Idaho courts.[9] There is no recent record of Idaho courts taking the lead in any significant public policy area and usurping the state legislature.

This culture of nonintervention by the courts into areas of public policy clearly aligns with the Jeffersonian view of the proper roles of the branches of government. As the courts are the farthest removed from the people, they should not be creating policy that directly affects the public.

According to the state constitution, Idaho judges and justices are to be elected by the people. However, the actual behavior of the public does not reflect the Jeffersonian principle of the people having a direct say in who occupies the benches of state courts. Instead the people and the officeholders behave more like Hamilton would have preferred.

As noted earlier, for an entire generation the justices of the state supreme court did not run in contested elections. Justices would retire during their term and allow the governor to appoint a replacement. When the term was completed, the justices did not face opposition. There was thus a de facto lifetime term for justices, with appointment as the means of selection. Magistrate judges already are appointed and only run in retention elections. The change to a Missouri Plan style of selection for these magistrate judges was legislated in 1973, showing an inclination, at least at that time, to move away from the election of members of the judiciary. Since the selection of magistrates in this manner has not changed, it can be assumed there is no public hue and cry about the procedure.

There is another twist to judicial elections in Idaho. The votes for judges and justices are not held during the general election in November but during primary elections, usually in May. Primary elections typically see only about a third of the registered voters going to the polls, while the turnout for general elections tends to be closer to 50 percent. With the Republican Party in Idaho closing its primaries (i.e., requiring a voter to be registered in the Republican Party to vote in the Republican primary), turnout in the primaries tends to decline even further. Nonaffiliated voters and of course those registered in other parties can vote for judicial candidates even if the voter cannot cast a vote for anyone running for nonjudicial offices.

Idaho standards also circumscribe the activities of judicial elections. The Idaho Code of Judicial Conduct for Judges strictly forbids candidates from making statements on cases that may come before the court in the future. This prohibition basically has candidates, at least in public, being limited to discussing their qualifications and résumés. This type of public participation does not fit the Jeffersonian mold.

In 2002 an extensive voter survey concerning judicial elections in Idaho found that more than two-thirds of respondents supported moving from elections to a merit-based Missouri Plan style of selecting judges. The survey question proposed that the Judicial Council would recommend "qualified" candidates for the governor to appoint. Those appointed would eventually have to run in a retention election.[10] This research supports the contention that Idahoans believe that the judiciary, at least in how jurists are selected, should be more in line with Hamilton's principles.

Like the other branches of the state government, the Idaho judiciary is a paradox when viewed in the light of petit-ideology. Its structure is Hamiltonian because it is unified and controlled by the state supreme court, and it is thus clearly aristocratic and hierarchical in nature. Conversely, however, since the judges and justices are "elected by the electors of the state at large," as spelled out in the state constitution and supported overwhelmingly at the constitutional convention, the state judiciary clearly reflects a Jeffersonian approach that relies on the wisdom of the people to staff the courts. The cultural beliefs and behavior of the people of Idaho are also in conflict with the principles reflected in the state's judicial structures. The courts do not venture into the realm of public policy often and rarely make decisions that affect the rights of the citizens of the state. The courts acquiesce to the more popularly elected state legislature to take the lead on public policy decisions, a nod to the Jeffersonian belief in the need for the supremacy of the legislature. However, leaning more toward the Hamiltonian vision of a judiciary detached from the passions of the public, Idaho judicial elections are often not contested, and the public, according to a survey, would prefer judges and justices in the state to be appointed on merit. The conflict between the two poles of petit-ideology permeates the structure and culture of the Idaho judiciary much as it does throughout the rest of the state government and among the people of the state.

CHAPTER SEVEN

Local Government

THE LILLIPUTIANS OF IDAHO

On Tuesday, May 19, 2015, voters in and around Kuna, Idaho, went to the polls to vote on creating a recreation district. The district, which would have the power to levy taxes on property owners within its boundaries, was conceived as a means to raise money to accumulate and provide operating funds for a pool and recreation facility. A simple majority vote would create the district, though a two-thirds majority would be needed to float a bond to pay for the construction of the facility. The district would include fewer than twenty thousand persons.[1] In the end voters chose not to create the district. This district would have been every bit as much a unit of local government as any city or county.

Recalling Jonathan Swift's political satire *Gulliver's Travels*, one can view the state government in Idaho as Gulliver and the local governments as the people from Lilliput. Lilliputians, besides literally being inhabitants of Lilliput, were illiberal, insular, narrow, little, narrow-minded, parochial, petty, picayune, provincial, and sectarian.[2] Local government at times displays all of these characteristics. In Idaho every taxing district is in actuality a form of local government. As of 2013, according to the Idaho State Tax Commission's annual report, there were 1,114 taxing districts in Idaho, though only 964 actually levied taxes during that year.[3] This is a large number of often tiny organizations that can stymie the larger though typically more virtuous Gulliver of state government. In effect the Hamiltonian state government must contend with the numerous Jeffersonian local government entities.

SINGLE-PURPOSE LOCAL GOVERNMENTS

When most people think of local government, they have cities and counties in mind. In most states, and especially Idaho, single-purpose districts greatly outnumber the general-purpose variety of municipalities and counties. The state's single-purpose districts (called "special districts" in Idaho) outnumber the general-purpose districts five to one. Why does Idaho have so many single-purpose districts?

As the name implies, single-purpose districts concentrate on a primary service, while a municipality provides a multitude of services to the public. As of 2014, Idaho's Legislative Services Office counted 1,556 taxing districts in the state, with 245 being city or county districts and 1,311 being single-purpose districts. These special districts include cemetery maintenance districts, mosquito abatement districts, fire protection districts, highway districts, irrigation districts, and soil conservation districts, as well as urban renewal districts, which are among the most recent and the most controversial.[4]

As the example of the recreation district around Kuna shows, there are a number of advantages to these single-purpose or special districts. One of the primary purposes of special districts is to try to lay the cost of services on those who benefit from those services. Although this effort to pinpoint levies to users is never going to be perfect, it is easier with districts created for a single purpose. Taxes can be collected from just those who use a specific water or irrigation system or those affected by mosquitoes, although insects do not respect district lines. Some of these services overlap traditional local government (i.e., city and county), making those general-purpose entities less efficient in solving the problems the special districts exclusively address. Special districts are not panaceas for these issues, though. As opponents of the Kuna Recreation District noted, not everyone who would use the recreation facility would be part of the district—the center would sell memberships—and some in the district would not use the new center.[5]

Based on ideals that date back to the Progressive Era, special districts are a means to prevent corruption in city and county governments from affecting services that many feel should not be politicized. This is especially true for school districts, and thus single-purpose districts are quite common in large urban areas, especially where, unlike Idaho, city and county elections are partisan affairs. Special districts are seen as oases of clean government separated from the arid deserts of corrupt urban machines, regardless of the truth to these characterizations or the effectiveness of the methods.

Special districts are also effective means for raising funds outside the framework of general-purpose governments. Levies or bonds designated for a particular purpose, such as a new school or highway, may be much more palatable to voters than taxes that end up in a pool used for myriad unseen expenditures that many might find less palatable.

Lastly, single-purpose special districts are sometimes promoted as being less costly than traditional governing bodies. Members of the governing board, typically titled commissioners or supervisors, are not paid and accomplish their mission with a skeleton staff. Special districts are often run on a shoestring, thus making them popular among fiscal conservatives.

But special districts are not perfect and have a number of shortcomings. The last advantage noted above was low cost, but single-purpose governments can also be inefficient and thus costly. Small governmental entities cannot take advantage of economies of scale and often duplicate operations (e.g., payroll, tax collection) that are also performed by other districts or levels of government. Inefficiencies also accrue to districts that have no permanent staff and are forced to hire contractors on an ad hoc basis.

The large number of districts performing discrete functions also leads to a lack of coordination. Efficiencies are created when two organizations handle complementary services, whether based on function or geography. In Idaho highway districts on occasion will quarrel with municipal and county governments as each governmental entity attempts to attain similar goals through different means.

Special districts can also be inefficient due to their single-purpose nature. When a district has a surplus of funds, it cannot direct the resources to other projects or functions. Special districts may overinvest in infrastructure or take on projects that are of questionable effectiveness since the funds are not fungible. A multipurpose or general district, such as a city or county, can more easily channel resources to higher-priority projects.

Finally, single-purpose districts tend to be invisible to most members of the public. To a lesser extent with school districts and their boards, commissioners or supervisors of most districts are unknown to the public. Candidates and voters pay little attention to most elections. Voter turnout for school board elections in Idaho, a state with higher than average turnout, is sometimes below 10 percent. When the public is not aware of the workings of a governmental district, accountability is typically lacking.

The abundance of single-purpose districts in Idaho has proved to be inefficient and invisible despite claims of effectiveness. The small districts often exhibit the worst traits of the Lilliputians.

THE BEST-KNOWN SINGLE-PURPOSE DISTRICTS: SCHOOLS

According to the Idaho State Department of Education, in 2014, there were 115 public school districts in Idaho, with a total of 280,000 students in attendance. On average there are more than 2,400 students per district and fewer than 13,000 inhabitants per district. School districts in some counties spend almost as much as the county and all of the cities in the county combined (e.g., Ada County), and some spend even more than that combined total (e.g., Canyon County).[6] Public schools tend to have high fixed costs. The smaller districts in the state have difficulty funding infrastructure. Although the state government provides some funding to local school districts, the community bears most of the burden of funding its schools.

School districts, as well as other special-purpose districts, struggle to find sufficient funding sources. Most of the resources available to schools are provided by the state government. This trend was accelerated when the legislature, in an extraordinary session, had the state assume responsibility for most of the maintenance and operations costs for public schools. This legislation was intended to lower the schools' dependence on property taxes, and in turn it increased the state's sales tax from 5 to 6 percent. Three years later, with the onset of the Great Recession, the state collected less revenue and reduced the amount of funding directed to the school districts. Relying on state funding for schools leaves the districts at the whim of the state legislature and the vagaries of the economy. Local property taxes mitigate some of these funding problems but open up still others.

The only other source of funds for local schools, as well as other single-purpose districts, is property taxes. Tax payments based on the assessed value of real estate tend to be a steadier form of revenue, being less affected by disturbances in the economy. This relative stability is seen as the paramount advantage of the property tax; however, this was not the case during the Great Recession, as property values plummeted along with the other aspects of the economy. Dependence on local property taxes for funding has many other tribulations for both the districts and those who own property within the district.

For example, property taxes are typically regressive. As one's income decreases, the percentage of that income that must be used to pay the tax increases. Typically the more one earns, the higher the value of the property that is purchased, yet this relationship does not always conform to reality. This is especially true with retirees. Although their income has decreased after retirement, the value of their home and thus their property tax does not decrease. The property tax is not based on the taxpayer's ability to pay.

Using local property taxes for funding also creates inequities among districts. As the property tax is based on assessed values within the district, districts with more valuable real estate will have greater access to resources for their schools. School districts throughout the country as well as in Idaho have great discrepancies in their funding. Such inequities among resources for districts often translate into very unequal educational opportunities among districts.

This problem is often exacerbated during poor economic times, when state funding is reduced. With less funding from the state, districts have to turn more to property taxes to make up for the lost revenue. This is done in Idaho through supplemental levies. Voters within the district must approve additional property taxes to help fund the schools in their district. These votes are not automatic and can lead to even greater resource disparity among districts. According to the Idaho Center for Fiscal Policy, the amount of money school districts collected from supplemental override levies nearly doubled between 2007 and 2013.[7] As schools rely more on the state legislature for funding, declines in the economy have a greater impact on district budgets.

GENERAL-PURPOSE LOCAL GOVERNMENT: COUNTIES

Counties are the basic administrative unit in almost every state. States created counties to more efficiently provide basic services to the public.

Although some counties, especially in the Midwest, were rationally created and resemble perfectly square blocks, Idaho and most states have a haphazard history of creating, dividing, and shaping their counties. Idaho now has forty-four counties, and they range in population from more than four hundred thousand (Ada County) to under a thousand (Clark County), yet the structure of each county government is the same. One structure does not quite fit all when it comes to Idaho counties.

Each county has a board of three commissioners elected for alternating four- and two-year terms. Although the entire county votes in the election for all three commissioners (i.e., at large), the county is divided into three districts and each commissioner must represent one of the three districts. Commissioners perform the legislative function, including budgeting, for the county, though they also share limited administrative and executive functions with the other elected officials for the county. This is where most conflict develops in county government: elected commissioners trying to "run" the county government even though they share powers with other independently elected county officials.

Besides the commissioners, each county elects six other officials: clerk, treasurer, assessor, sheriff, coroner, and prosecuting attorney. All are elected independently and typically act independently. These positions are four-year terms, and candidates run in partisan elections, as do the commissioners. Each and every county in Idaho has these same offices regardless of the geographic size of the county or the number of inhabitants.

Only one position requires a special prerequisite for office—the prosecuting attorney must be licensed to practice law in Idaho. Even though only that one position has a prerequisite, counties have trouble filling some posts. Prosecuting attorney is the most difficult post to fill, and some counties thus share or contract out the service. Coroners need no special training and have to contract out services if a major case arises. The basic county structure obviously doesn't suit all counties.

The state constitution was amended in 1994 to allow counties to implement optional forms of county government. In accordance with the amendment, the state legislature two years later passed enacting legislation providing for alternative forms of government for the counties and a mechanism for counties to create a charter unique to the specific county. The charter could change the form of government, but it could not change any of the other powers of the county government. Most of the potential changes affected the commissioners.

If the charter is approved by the voters in the county, the size of the board of commissioners could be increased to five or seven. To solve the problem of unclear lines of demarcation between the legislative and executive functions of the commission, these large boards could create an executive board of its members.

Two other methods to more clearly delineate the legislative and executive powers of the commissioners are also permitted. Regardless of the size of the board, the charter can call for a single elected executive or a single manager appointed by the commission. This structure most closely resembles the different types of structures of cities, described below.

The charter form of county government also permits changes to the other uniform elected positions in each county. The positions other than commissioners may be eliminated completely, changed to selection by appointment, have their terms changed, or even have the powers divided differently. As long as the county continues to perform all of the functions assigned to it by the state, the legislation provides a wide range of means to accomplish these tasks. To handle the problem of small counties not being able to find people to serve in mandated positions, counties are allowed to combine positions with other counties as long as the voters in both counties agree.

To change a county government organization, the voters must approve a commission to draft a charter. The commission is limited to four years before it is dissolved. A charter created by a commission must be placed before the voters before it is enacted. Several Idaho counties have created commissions, and some of the commissions have drafted charters. No charter to change the structure of county government has been ratified by the voters of any county. The public seems to prefer their current form of county government despite its faults.

County government in Idaho, with its warring factions of commissioners versus independently elected officials, fits many of the traits exhibited in Lilliput. The officials are parochial, even toward their own positions, petty in regard to their turf, and illiberal, as the county government itself is often the most resistant to change. The county is supposed to assist the state government in the governance of the state. The one-size-fits-all county structure at times seems more of a hindrance, tying down the state, than functioning as tiny helpers for Gulliver.

GENERAL-PURPOSE LOCAL GOVERNMENT: CITIES

Once one gets below the state and the county level, the only general-purpose form of local government in Idaho is the city. Some, especially those from the East Coast, would claim Idaho does not have any cities, just small towns and maybe villages. The diversity of size among communities in Idaho—Boise with more than two hundred thousand and Warm River in Fremont County with three residents—is not matched by any diversity in the categorizing or labeling of communities in Idaho. Every municipality in Idaho is referred to as a city regardless of the geographic size or the number of residents.

Only three cities received charters under the territorial government in Idaho: Boise, Lewiston, and Bellevue. Boise and Lewiston have since abandoned their charters in favor of the uniform law covering all other cities. Bellevue, in Blaine County, thus remains the only city in Idaho that is governed under a territorial charter, does not conform to the State Municipal Code, and must have any changes to the charter approved by the state legislature.[8] Although every city does not have the exact same structure, as is the case with the counties, the differences, despite size, are few and far between.

There are only two accepted forms of government allowed for cities in Idaho, and all but three cities in Idaho operate under a mayor-council system. The mayor and members of the council are chosen by voters in nonpartisan elections for four-year terms. Idaho cities do have the power to set the size of the city council at either four or six members. This formal system favors a relatively strong mayor, one who functions as the chief executive of the city and who also presides over the council meetings. Although casting votes only when needed to break ties, the mayor, since the position is full-time while the council seats are only part-time positions, wields power over the council due to expertise and knowledge. This form of government is shared by cities of various sizes throughout the state, with the only option being the size of the council.

Three Idaho cities—Lewiston, Twin Falls, and McCall—have opted for a manager-council form of government. Pocatello also used this structure for about thirty-five years before returning to the mayor-council form in 1985.[9] Under the manager-council system the city council is chosen in a nonpartisan election, just as in the mayor-council system, but the council appoints a city manager to perform all of the administrative functions for the city. The manager acts, at least from an administrative standpoint, as the mayor. There is technically a mayor under this system, but he or she is only a member chosen from among the council to preside over meetings. The mayor in this system votes on all matters.

There is no clear correlation between which cities in Idaho use the manager-council system. Similar to counties, cities are given some leeway in determining their form of government, but in general they do not choose to avail themselves of this choice. In Idaho the cities stumble along, fighting with the state and among themselves more often than working to aid their residents.

LOCAL GOVERNMENT ELECTIONS

Counties hold their elections in even-numbered years, and they are partisan affairs just like other state and national contests. Cities and special districts have elections in odd-numbered years or at nontraditional times (i.e., not in November) with candidates not identified by party labels. A further investigation into the selection process of these less traditional elections is warranted.

The characteristics of elections for cities and special districts in Idaho are descended from the Progressive Era of the early twentieth century in reaction to urban political machines. Although these machines in the traditional sense are rare in the current American political system, these reforms have endured.

A political "machine" can be thought of as a local political party capable of organizing to consistently deliver the vote for its candidates. The machine is typically held together by the prospect of material rewards to workers for their loyalty.[10] Additional advantages of a political machine, at least to those within its hierarchy, included a structure of opportunity for ambitious young men without formal education who could work their way up the party organization. This was seen by some as one of the only avenues for most immigrants to advance within society.

The Progressives saw the more venal side to urban political machines. Held together by favors distributed to loyal members of the party, including those who merely voted for the machine candidates, the gifts had only a limited impact on the often dire circumstances of the poor and mostly immigrant populations of the inner cities of the late nineteenth and early twentieth century.

Machines were notorious for their corruption. Most people are familiar with the old chestnuts about electoral corruption (e.g., voting early and often, voting despite being dead), but corruption and graft were endemic in the machine's relations with businesses and all levels of government. Many of the corrupt practices provided opportunities for at least some of the cogs in the machine to earn some illegal income.[11] Such flagrant violations of what many in "better society" saw as good government led to electoral and other reforms under the banner of the Progressive movement.

Many reforms instituted by the Progressives went beyond city government and included the Australian style or secret ballot, direct primaries, and the civil service system, which was the pet peeve of George Washington Plunkitt, the best-known spokesperson of New York City's Tammany Hall political machine.[12] Two Progressive Era reforms to local government affect Idaho to this day.

Progressives worked to remove party labels from local ballots as a means of reducing the influence of local party machines. This reform is still in place in as many as three-quarters of American cities. Ideally voters would decide on candidates based on the qualities of those candidates rather than according to which party the candidate and voter belonged. The lack of the party label removes an important cue to voters in local elections, which tend to be low-information affairs with voters scrambling for signs on how to vote. Nonpartisan elections often still have clear adherents from each party running for office even if the party name is not on the ballot. Wealthy and prominent candidates often have a distinct advantage in such elections, which was desirable to many Progressives.

Another vestige of the Progressive Era in Idaho local politics is at-large elections. Instead of dividing a city or special district into separate precincts or wards, the entire populace of the political entity votes for each position of a board, commission, or city council. This is different from what most people are familiar with when voting for Congress. The

Progressives believed that small wards could be controlled by the machine while the entire city could not. At-large elections have more recently been outlawed in some areas, as they erect a barrier to minorities in electing representatives.

Elections for local government in Idaho carry the vestiges of the Progressive war against political machines despite the generally weak nature of political parties in the state's history. The use of nonpartisan elections weakens the dominance of the Idaho Republican Party on the local level, but at-large elections raise a barrier to candidates who align more closely with the Democratic Party.

BOISE AND UBER: GULLIVER STRIKES BACK

While the local government Lilliputians can be troublesome and annoying to the state government Gulliver, in the end Dillon's Rule prevails. As described in more detail in chapter 10, on intergovernmental relations, Dillon's Rule is the premise that, since state government created the local governments, the state can also dictate to the locals. This rule was in play in 2015, when the ride-sharing enterprise Uber wished to establish itself in the city of Boise.

Uber began operating in Boise in 2014 on a free basis, since city ordinances did not recognize it as a legally functioning enterprise. The city council wanted to regulate Uber in much the way it did limousines and shuttles. With a delay in the actual enactment of the regulations, Uber took its case to the Idaho state legislature. Uber wrote its own law that would put it and other "transportation network companies" under the regulatory purview of the state.[13] The bill passed the state legislature and became law without Governor Otter's signature.

While many in Idaho, especially Jeffersonians, cringe at the national government "telling" the state what to do, many have no qualms with the state dictating to its local government appendages. This contradiction was voiced by Maryanne Jordan, who is a member of both the state senate and Boise City Council. "I've observed the frustrations that a lot of people in the [state] Senate have with the federal government usurping what they believe to be the authority of the state," Jordan said. "And so I'm hoping that they will see that this argument is a similar one."[14] As noted later, in the chapter on intergovernmental relations, where one stands on an issue depends on where one sits.

Although the Lilliputians may try to tie Gulliver down, eventually he holds the upper hand. The state, under Dillon's Rule, has complete authority over local governments and does not shy away from using its power. The cities, counties, and special districts can be an annoyance, but in the end Gulliver will prevail.

An examination of local government in Idaho again shows the tension between the ideals of the Jeffersonians and Hamiltonians. Those who prefer the Jeffersonian ideal wish to push public decisions down to the lowest governmental level possible. Local government solutions should be held paramount. This principle runs into the communitarian vision of the Hamiltonian side of petit-ideology, which wants to see commonality of policy throughout the state. The state government, supposedly filled with Jeffersonians, endeavors to limit the actions of local governments. The friction between the two sides of petit-ideology is present in the relationship between state and local governments much as it is throughout the state.

CHAPTER EIGHT

Interest Groups in Idaho

TRYING TO MEASURE INFLUENCE

Interest groups have fascinated political economists in the United States since James Madison and his ruminations on the mischief of factions. Through the years even the definition of an interest group has differed from study to study, and there is not even a clear consensus on the most appropriate term for such groups. (Have researchers finally abandoned use of the term "pressure groups"?) Students of Idaho politics seem equally fascinated by groups, as well as in trying to measure their influence and strength. From at least 1970 researchers have developed studies, with similar though divergent methodologies, that attempt to fully measure the influence of groups and how the influence of any one group has waxed or waned through the years. A stroll down the memory lane of interest group studies in Idaho will provide a better understanding of the impact various groups have had in the recent past while illuminating some of the murky corners of Idaho politics in general. Initially, a general review of how one might measure the strength of interest groups is needed. Interest groups, like traditional formal organizations within government, show the same tension between the Jeffersonian and Hamiltonian poles of petit-ideology.

HOW SHOULD ONE STUDY THE INFLUENCE OF INTEREST GROUPS?

Ideally a researcher studying any political entity would want to determine the entity's influence in the political realm. Influence is a consequence of power. In essence, then, the variable in need of measurement is power.

Power is usually seen as the ability to get someone to do something he or she would otherwise not do. The problem with measuring power is that measurement cannot be done directly, so alternatives must be pursued.

The next level of measurement of influence would be whether an entity is able to achieve its goals. This is defined as single-group power.[1] In theory this measure shows the ability of an entity to shape its environment to its own desires. One would merely have to compare the goals of a group with the public policy outputs to measure a percentage of success. In practice, scholars studying interest groups find this definition very difficult to test empirically. Interest groups do not often reveal their preferences to the public. Groups that announce goals publicly generally are directing propaganda toward their members and the public, not providing information to researchers. Without an honest declaration of goals, it is impossible to measure success.

In general there are three challenges to measuring the power or influence of interest groups. When studying any policy decision, many variables, some related to the group and others not, may affect the decision. Also, just because a group is highly visible does not necessarily mean that the group is influential. Lastly, what may look like influence by a group may merely be that the group has the same goals as policy makers.[2]

In studying interest groups on the state level, researchers have resorted to indirect measures of influence. The problem has been that prior methods have measured only one aspect of interest group strength at a time. Looking at a subject from various angles simultaneously provides a fuller picture and understanding of our subject.

Researchers in the past have typically looked at the reputational aspect of interest group strength.[3] Reputational measurement would determine which groups participants and observers feel are the most influential on the policy process and thus most effective. This aspect of strength is important, as perceived power may be as effective as actual power. This reputational strength is measured by three different methods: surveys of public officials, often with coordinated interviews; evaluations by political scientists; and literature reviews of popular and academic writings on the subject.[4]

A second facet of interest group power is electoral. The ability to influence the election of public officials indicates the power to impact the environment within which the group participates. Placing favorable actors into authority will assist the group in achieving its goals. Similar to other empirical measures, it is not practical to be able to determine which groups provided the specific resources that changed the outcome of an election from a candidate unfavorable to the group to one that was favorable. A group's influence from an electoral standpoint can be measured by the amount of money it contributes to the electoral process. Money is in many ways the most important resource in elections and makes for a reasonable unit of analysis for the measurement of an interest group's electoral influence.

A third aspect of interest group influence can be described as operational. Interest groups typically attempt to influence the outputs of government through lobbying. By providing legislators with information on how legislation will affect constituents, interest groups are able to influence the shape of legislation. Lobbying is done by explaining, cajoling, providing information, and, in general, trying to convince the official of the wisdom of the group's goals. Lobbying has often taken place in the hallways of the legislature, but meals and entertainment are also in the mix. Again, it is not practical to measure the exact influence a lobbyist has on any one legislator, much less on the legislature as a whole. Did the one conversation over dinner change the legislator's vote? Did that one vote change the outcome of the legislation? What can be measured is the amount of resources a group puts into lobbying legislators to enact legislation beneficial to the group and thus to assist the group in achieving its goals.

These three aspects provide the best means for measuring the influence of interest groups. The combination of lobbying and campaign contributions has been seen as effective. As one scholar notes, "Groups with the most reason to back up their contributions with intense lobbying were the most effective."[5] Groups seldom have just one method or characteristic that makes them effective. Early studies of interest groups in Idaho did not make use of all three means to measure interest group strength.

IDAHO INTEREST GROUPS IN THE LATE TWENTIETH CENTURY

Early studies of interest groups in Idaho have looked at the three aspects of group strength identified above, but no single study did so. These early studies, like studies of interest groups in other states, have been sporadic and inconsistent. With regard to Idaho after the turn of the twenty-first century, "there are no current surveys indicating interest group strength[,] but it is safe to say that dominance by a few groups is more difficult today in a more complex, growth-oriented state."[6]

Reputational

The most extensive early study of interest groups in Idaho was undertaken decades ago. The study included thirty-seven groups, chosen based on the authors' knowledge, previous research, and conversations with those familiar with groups in the state. Respondents, both state legislators and lobbyists, were asked to rank the fifteen groups that were the most influential in "obtaining legislative acceptance of their position."[7] Listings of groups were created based on the number of times the group was mentioned by a respondent.

Although some authors, such as Gary Moncrief, cite Sarah Morehouse's listing of influential interest groups in Idaho, her source is actually secondary, as well as older.[8] Morehouse's list is derived from Neal Peirce's 1972 study of western states. Peirce's work consisted of interviewing key actors in the state and conducting a review of secondary sources. Peirce's description of prominent groups was both general (e.g., stock raisers, mining interests, and forest industries) and specific (e.g., Idaho Power Company, Idaho Farm Bureau, the Mormon Church, and the Idaho Education Association).[9] Clive Thomas and Ronald Hrebenar began surveying political scientists in all fifty states, including Idaho, in 1985. Besides characterizing states by the overall impact of interest groups, their surveys asked the respondents to classify groups into one of five categories.[10] This categorization has been used in more recent studies of Idaho interest groups.

Electoral

A previous study in Idaho showed overall spending by political action committees (PACs) increased from $343,529 in the 1977–78 election cycle to $378,467 in the 1979–80 election cycle and to $683,514 in the 1981–82 cycle.[11] The top two committees represented labor interests, with the remainder principally associations and PACs created for single issues or campaigns.[12]

A later review of the top-spending PACs concentrated on the changes from 1992 to 2002. Spending in these years also showed the influence of labor and single-issue PACs, though James Weatherby and Randy Stapilus have concluded that labor's influence was reduced due to its overwhelming support of Democratic candidates who were not successful in their election bids.[13]

Operational

In the early 1980s a review of interest groups in Idaho examined the change in the number of lobbyists and the amount of spending by groups. The number of lobbyists for the period of 1977 to 1983 ranged from 258 to 298, for an average of 280.3. The number of lobbyists who reported expenditures to the secretary of state ranged from 130 in 1982 to 178 in 1977, for an average of 158.6 for the period. The total amount of spending by groups lobbying the state legislature ranged from $264,000 in 1977 to $105,000 in 1979, for an average of $155,700 for the period. Although the number of groups is large by both measures, the number of groups spending more than $1,000 on lobbying activities ranged from 26 to 43, for an average of 34.4.[14]

Other studies have examined the number of "registered interest organizations" within the state. Under this category the number of organizations increased from 110 in 1975 to 220 in 1980 to 263 in 1990. Idaho's 100 percent increase in registered interest organizations from 1975 to 1980 is higher than the national average increase of just over 75 percent. The 19.5 percent increase in the 1980s was much lower than the 71.5 percent increase seen on average in the rest of the country. Overall Idaho consistently has had fewer registered organizations than the national average (1975: 110 versus 195.57; 1980: 220 versus 342.36; 1990: 263 versus 587.04).[15]

CURRENT STUDIES OF INTEREST GROUPS IN IDAHO

Recent studies of interest groups in Idaho by this author have used aspects of earlier work and suggest that groups can gain influence by various means.

Reputational

Surveys of the members of the Idaho state legislature were conducted during the 2008, 2010, 2012, and 2014 sessions. The surveys listed up to twenty-nine interest groups, and state legislators were asked to label each group according to one of the following categories:

1. Organizations that have been consistently active and effective at obtaining legislative acceptance of their position over the past two years

2. Organizations that are rising in power but have not met the consistency or effectiveness of the first rank

3. Organizations that have fallen from the top rank of consistency and effectiveness

4. Organizations that are consistently active but seldom effective

5. Organizations that are not consistently active but are effective on the occasions when they are active

This typology is similar to what Thomas and Hrebenar have used in their surveys of political scientists across the fifty states.[16]

No extensive empirical analysis was performed on the data. Other studies in this area and others with much larger numbers of respondents do not employ quantitative analysis that is complex or elaborate. As Michael Gorges has pointed out, "Elaborate quantitative analyses (regression, etc.) may be unnecessary for most interest group studies."[17]

Electoral

Beginning with the 2004 and 2006 election cycles, information was obtained on political committee expenditures.[18] The information is based on the campaign financial disclosure report that political committees must complete for the Office of the Secretary of State at various times during the electoral cycle. The public summary report of this information is compiled by the secretary of state's staff.[19] Political committees do not always correspond exactly with interest groups identified by other measures. During the analysis of the results, committees were aligned with groups based on a review of the contributors and discussions with those who participate in the activities of the groups.

Operational

The operational measure of interest group strength is related to the amount of financial resources dedicated to lobbying. The State of Idaho requires each lobbyist to report spending during each month that the state legislature is in session and to submit an annual report if lobbying the legislature, while those registered to lobby the executive branch are required to file only a semiannual and a final annual report.[20] The Office of the Secretary of State tallies the expenditures and summarizes the material by employer (i.e., interest group) and lobbyist. Most of the information used was the data sorted by employer, though references to the specific lobbyist and actual report were indicated when necessary.

ANALYSIS OF SURVEY RESULTS

Comparing reputational results with the past (specifically the Weatherby and Nichols study) showed that four groups made the top ten in both the past and the present: Associated Taxpayers of Idaho, the Association of Idaho Cities, the Idaho Association of Commerce and Industry (previously known as Associated Industries of Idaho), and Idaho Power.[21] Associated General Contractors was lower on the list in the past, while the Idaho Education Association, Idaho Cattle Association (previously known as the Idaho Cattlemen's Association), and Idaho Farm Bureau were in the top ten in 1970 but not among the ten groups receiving the most votes in category 1 in the recent surveys.

An examination of the electoral activity of groups currently viewed by legislators as active and effective shows that most do not even make contributions to candidates. Two groups represent levels of the state government (Idaho Association of Counties, Association of Idaho Cities), one group (Idaho Food Producers) is an umbrella organization whose members make electoral contributions separately, and another group (Associated Taxpayers of Idaho) wants to retain its independent reputation and thus does not as a rule contribute to candidates. The utility (Idaho Power) makes contributions only to candidates campaigning for positions at the national level of government.

A comparison with campaign spending of decades ago shows some overlap. In the late 1970s and early 1980s the Idaho Education Association, Idaho Association of Commerce and Industry, and the Idaho Realtors Association were also near the top of contributors, but the AFL-CIO and Morrison Knudson have greatly reduced campaign contributions since that time.[22] A significant change from 2008 to 2014 has been the drop in influence and electoral activity by the Idaho Association of Realtors and the Associated General Contractors. Based on the reduction of real estate activity in the state during this period, the drop in those groups' activity seems logical.

There is a much closer relationship between reputational measures of strength and operational spending on lobbying. Most of the top reputational groups (e.g., Idaho Association of Counties, Idaho Association of Commerce and Industry, and Idaho Power) are also typically among those that spend the most on lobbying efforts. Again, there were two outliers (i.e., high reputation but low lobbying spending) for similar reasons, as was the case with the electoral spending measure. The Associated Taxpayers of Idaho does not spend any money on lobbying (in order to retain its independence), while Idaho Food Producers has only an insignificant lobbying budget because it is an umbrella group whose members lobby on their own.

In comparison with lobbying spending in the 1970s and 1980s, there is little overlap between which groups spend the most on lobbying and how much these groups spend. The total amount spent on lobbying in 1983 was just short of $138,000.[23] The total spent in 2006 was almost $870,000. Idaho Power alone spent almost $180,000 on lobbying in 2006. The number of groups spending a significant amount on lobbying also increased. In 1983 forty groups spent at least $1,000 on lobbying.[24] In 2006, however, 101 groups spent at least that much.

These findings leave more questions than answers: Why do some groups have the reputation for effectiveness yet spend little on campaign contributions or lobbying? Why are some of the highest-spending groups not seen as the most effective? Is there another factor that helps explain effectiveness?

THE EFFECT OF LOBBYISTS AND CONSTITUENTS

There seems to be no clear relationship among the three means of measuring interest group influence. Although there is overlap among some groups in each category, there are clear anomalies. The group rated as active and effective by more legislators than any other group (Associated Taxpayers of Idaho) does not spend any money operationally or electorally. Some of the groups that are the largest spenders operationally and electorally are not rated highly by legislators. There must be another factor, or factors, that can explain the effectiveness of groups besides who they represent, how much money they spend on lobbying, and how much they spend on contributions to candidates.

Interviews with more than twenty-five lobbyists, legislators, members of the media, and government officials in the legislative and executive branches were conducted to determine why some groups were more effective than others for reasons beyond those studied. These interviews were conducted during the legislative session of 2008. The interviews were mostly open-ended, with participants given great latitude on how they wanted to answer the general questions on interest groups, lobbying, and lobbyists presented to them. The interviews were not recorded and no promises of anonymity were granted.[25]

Almost all respondents, without prompting, noted the importance of the individual lobbyist in determining the effectiveness of the group in attaining the group's desired goals. This was an expected response from the lobbyists, but it was repeated by those in every category. Although the group that the lobbyist represents plays a role in the group's success, the individual representing the group to government officials is still an important factor. Hiring a different lobbyist could change the group's ability to succeed.

The key ingredient of a successful lobbyist is credibility. Lobbyists whom legislators or executive branch officials believe are not providing credible or useful information will not be effective. Credibility is seen by most as never misrepresenting the issues or positions of one's clients or others. Nothing incorrect can be provided to officials without a loss of credibility. Honesty is only the lowest common denominator for success. One must not "spin" the information even if the information is factually correct. Legislators in particular expect clear information about not only the position of the lobbyist's group but also who is on the other side of an issue and what are the other side's best arguments. As a provider of information, the lobbyist must present the information in a truthful and balanced manner to have the greatest success.

Credibility is important because in the end the lobbyist is principally a resource for legislators. The lobbyist provides information on issues, constituents, and other lawmakers. This is especially important in the Idaho state legislature because the members are not full-time legislators. Belonging to a "citizen" legislature and having little to no staff, the members of the Idaho legislature rely on lobbyists to perform many of the functions that are done in other venues by paid staffers or the legislators themselves. This relationship provides the opportunity for significant influence by lobbyists on the public policy of the state.

These comments on lobbyists should not discount the importance of the interest group's constituency to the overall success of that group and its lobbyists. Who a group represents can be a critical factor in its ability to influence legislators. From the study of the three factors and interviews, it is apparent that three types of groups benefit the most from their constituents: general business (e.g., chambers of commerce), teachers, and governmental units. Business groups that represent a broad range of industries tend to have representatives in many districts and thus relationships with many legislators. Teachers, especially the teachers' union, can also be effective due to their dispersion throughout the state. While the Idaho Education Association is not always seen as consistently successful in the legislative arena, teachers can, as individuals and not as members of a union, be as effective as any group given their prominence in the local community. Other governmental units (e.g., cities, counties) have a great deal of influence on the state government. Some attribute this influence to the similarity in the nature of their work, while others point to their shared background; many legislators used to be city and county officials and thus identify with the group. Who a group represents, how the group is organized, and who represents the group can be more important to a group's success than other factors.

Through the years and various studies, interest group activity in Idaho has not been shown to be significantly different from what exists in other states or in other levels of government. Since the state legislature is not professional (i.e., not a full-time undertaking for the elected members), lobbyists play a significant role in the functioning of government within the state. The groups seen as the most influential do not achieve this influence merely through spending on candidates and lobbying. The skill of the lobbyist and the character of members of the interest group seem to affect the ability of groups to shape government policy as much or more than any other factor.

Interest groups, with their narrow perspective, are the bane of the Hamiltonians. Instead of striving for the interests of whole of society, interest groups focus on their own desires over the needs of society. Only a pluralist who believes that the aggregation of various interests morphs into the common interest would see the collective benefit of interest group behavior. Jeffersonians then, in the world of interest groups, are the pluralists of petit-ideology.

CHAPTER NINE

Political Parties

WHAT'S THE MATTER WITH IDAHO?

Idaho is considered one of the "reddest" states in the country, meaning it votes overwhelmingly Republican. For example, after the election of 2014 all state executive offices were held by Republicans, all four members of the U.S. Congress from Idaho were Republicans, and exactly 80 percent of members of both the state house and state senate were Republicans. Since 1994 only one Democrat, Walt Minnick, has won a seat in Congress from Idaho (he was elected as representative to the First District in 2008 and 2010). No Democrat has won a U.S. Senate seat since Frank Church in 1974, and no Democrat has been elected governor since Cecil Andrus in 1990. No Democrat running for president has carried the state of Idaho since Lyndon Johnson in 1964; Bill Clinton came within seven thousand votes (just over 1 percent of the vote) of coming in third in 1992. Republican presidential nominee Mitt Romney received a higher percentage of votes in Idaho in the 2012 election than any other state besides Utah and Wyoming.

Idaho has not always been dominated by the Republican Party. A short review of the parties through Idaho's history will show many instances of, if not Democratic dominance, at least competitiveness between the two parties. Why has Idaho become such a Republican state? Three theories are posited here, with the last conclusion based on petit-ideology and a comparison of Idaho to Kansas.

AN ABBREVIATED HISTORY OF POLITICAL PARTIES IN IDAHO

A detailed review of the history of the Republican and Democratic parties in Idaho is beyond the scope of this book.[1] However, a brief overview of Idaho political party competition before the 1990s should shed some light on how the state has achieved its single-party status.

Idaho's origins are embedded in conflicts between the Democratic and Republican Parties. The Idaho Territory, which included what is now Wyoming and Montana along with Idaho, was created by Abraham Lincoln in 1863 and initially supported the Union and Republicans. The immigration of miners during the Civil War and Confederate sympathizers after the war turned the state into a stronghold of the Democrats. A shift of Mormon voters from Utah to Idaho, and their predilection for voting Democratic at the time, made Idaho solidly Democratic until 1882. It was the Mormon vote that would soon lead to the fall of the Democrats in Idaho.

Candidates in the 1880s began to run in the Idaho Territory specifically as "anti-Mormon" and in opposition to the Democratic Party. Some ran as members of the "Independent Anti-Mormon Party." Virulent hatred of members of the Church of Latter-day Saints reached its climax in 1885 with laws that prevented Mormons from voting, holding office, or serving on a jury. This anti-Mormon fervor caused the state to swing back to the Republicans and allowed it to gain admission to the Union in 1890.

After statehood a new political player joined the scene: the populists. Based on fervid Jeffersonian values of an aversion to big government and big business, the populists were naturally accepted in Idaho among the miners and settlers who were characteristically individualistic. The populists never dominated the state and had limited impact across the nation, but they helped stir up traditional party politics in Idaho such that neither party was dominant for the period leading up to the twentieth century. The populist experiment did lead to the strength of the Progressive movement in Idaho.

The early twentieth century saw labor strife and violence become pervasive in Idaho, and labor activism fueled an alliance between miners and farmers that was socialist in nature. The Socialist Party itself elected a member to the state senate in 1914, but the party never became a significant factor in state politics. Various movements for government ownership of utilities, railroads, and banks emerged, but none would be organized well enough to have any true electoral strength. Idaho in the 1920s, like the rest of the country, fell into a comfortable alliance with the Republican Party, though the country's first religiously observant Jewish governor, Moses Alexander, a Democrat, was elected in 1918 and served for four years.

The Great Depression changed the partisan balance in Idaho just as it did in the rest of the country. Another Democrat, C. Ben Ross, was elected governor in 1930.[2] It is thought that his election was based more on his personal charisma and electoral appeal than his party, as the Democrats picked up few seats in the legislature that year. Ross, with his populist spirit and close ties to farmers and labor, enacted his own miniature version of the New Deal in Idaho during the 1930s. He pushed a sales tax into law and was seen as the political power of the state. Ross's problem was that he made enemies within the Democratic Party, and when he decided to move on from governor, Ross tangled with Idaho's lion: incumbent U.S. senator William Borah. The populist/agrarian movement within the state was still strong but was not based on the traditional partisan divide. In their senatorial election Borah and Ross fought over the Progressive voters in the state, with Borah, the Republican, being triumphant. The Democrats, led by Compton White and the brothers Brazilla and Chase Clark, held on to power through the decade, but as the economy improved, so did prospects for the Republicans.

The next decade saw the positions for governor and seats in the U.S. Senate and House shift between the parties. With the economic upturn and World War II, Idaho turned away from its populist and progressive roots, with one exception: Glen Taylor.[3] Taylor is one of the truly unique characters in Idaho political history. He was elected to the U.S. Senate after seeing Ross campaign for governor. Taylor was as much an entertainer as he was a politician. His campaign style included having his family perform musical numbers before his campaign events and riding a horse across the state in 1942 because of gasoline and rubber rationing. Taylor was a radical; his proposal "Plenty for All" was similar to the "Share the Wealth" theory of agrarian populism advocated by Huey Long under the banner of "Every Man's a King." It was actually the conservatism of the Democratic Party that first pushed Taylor out of the Senate. He would go on to be the vice presidential candidate on the ticket with Henry Wallace of the Progressive Party in 1948. Taylor's last campaign led to a narrow defeat in the Democratic primary for U.S. Senate by a young upstart, Frank Church. Taylor contended that Church stole the election, but he could never conclusively prove his claims. Incredibly Taylor eventually moved to California and started a company that made toupees. In a blurb that appears on Taylor's autobiography the *San Francisco Chronicle* noted that "Glen Taylor may well have been the most honest man in American politics this century." Although politics in Idaho was competitive and rather boring in the middle decades of the twentieth century, Glen Taylor, a remnant of the populist Jeffersonian roots of the Democratic Party, provided entertainment to a rather dull party system.

Although Idaho is not known for robust party organizations or machines in the urban sense, the parties were controlled by political machines dominated by single individuals during much of the twentieth century. Lloyd Adams, from Rexburg, controlled much of the Republican Party political activity for decades, though he was pragmatic enough to work with Democrats like Ross. During fifty years of influence behind the scenes of Idaho politics and the Republican Party, Adams has been considered "the most effective lobbyist and political engineer Idaho has ever had."[4] Adams's Democratic counterpart was Tom Boise. Boise controlled the Democratic machine centered in Lewiston. A former Republican, Tom Boise supported conservative Democrats and was a fervent advocate for gambling in the state. Although he effectively controlled much of the Democratic Party in the 1950s when it was flourishing, Boise would finally be overthrown by the two young, more liberal Democratic leaders: Cecil Andrus and Frank Church.[5]

Part of the success of the Democratic Party in Idaho before 1994 and part of its failure after 1994 can be traced to its two most successful politicians. Frank Church and Cecil Andrus won many elections and became revered figures for the Democrats in the state. The two constitute most of the story of the party from the end of the 1950s until 1994. Although both were extremely successful and popular, the party was never able to extend that success or popularity over to the party itself.

While Church and Andrus were the giants of the Democratic Party, the Republicans were wrestling between the Hamiltonians and Jeffersonians in their party. Whether it was Smylie and Samuelson or Simms and

McClure, most of the 1960s and 1970s featured the Republicans in Idaho winning most of the positions but never attaining complete dominance. The 1990s began with an election that seemed to place the Democrats on the verge of becoming the majority party in the state.

The 1990 election was not a clean sweep for the Democrats, but it was very successful. Although Larry Craig won the race for the U.S. Senate for the Republicans, Democrats (Larry LaRocco and Richard Stallings) won both U.S. House seats. In the statewide races for the Democrats, Andrus was reelected governor, collecting more than two-thirds of the vote; Larry Echo Hawk was elected attorney general; and J. D. Williams was chosen as state auditor. The only state office the Democrats contested and lost was treasurer. (Oddly the Democrats ran no candidates for lieutenant governor, secretary of state, or superintendent of public instruction.) Although the Democrats had not had control of either chamber of the state legislature since the election of 1958, in 1990 the state senate was evenly split with twenty-one senators of each party. By 1994 the Idaho Democratic Party electorally would be in shambles.

Despite fielding what the Democrats termed a "dream ticket" in 1994, they went on to lose both U.S. House seats, including that of incumbent Larry LaRocco, and all of the statewide offices save that of state auditor, which incumbent J. D. Williams won by less than 1 percent, or four thousand votes. The Democrats went from twenty-one state senators in 1991 to a mere eight after the 1994 election, while their numbers in the state house dropped from twenty-eight to thirteen. The raw numbers look worse because the legislature reduced its numbers due to reapportionment, from forty-two to thirty-five senators and from eighty-four to seventy representatives. Still, the percentage of Democratic senators dropped from 50 percent in 1991 to under 23 percent in 1995, and the proportion of Democratic representatives went from one-third of the chamber to just over one in six. The Democratic Party in the Idaho state legislature hit its nadir after the 2000 election, which left only three Democrats in the thirty-five-member state senate and only nine Democrats in the state house, which had a total of seventy representatives.

Why has the Democratic Party, while never a political juggernaut in Idaho, been relegated to this minority status and is now seldom competitive in statewide elections? Three theories are proposed on why this situation has come about: one based on organization, another on economic demographics, and the last involving petit-ideology and a comparison of Idaho with Kansas. So, what's the matter with Idaho?

ORGANIZATION: PARTY VERSUS PERSONAL

One could argue that the rise of a dominant Republican Party in Idaho can be traced to one person: Phil Batt. If party organization and recruiting people to work on the nuts and bolts of the party is the ticket to winning elections, then Batt is the person most responsible for the ascendancy of Republicans in modern-day Idaho.

Batt described the 1990 election as the Republican Party's worst results in decades. Subsequently he volunteered to be state chair for the party. While others licked their wounds, Phil Batt went about making the Idaho Republican Party a machine that could rarely be beat.

In his book *The Compleat Phil Batt* the man who would one day be governor describes his philosophy on building a party organization. Traveling throughout the state, Batt recruited and trained the foot soldiers necessary to win campaigns. His workshops for the committee members he had recruited throughout the state emphasized the commonality of Republican voters and not what divided them.[6] Ever the Wilsonian, Batt looked for pragmatic, not ideological, methods to strengthen his party.

Batt was not someone to leave the heavy lifting of campaigning to others. He believed that if Idaho was a Republican state, then it should elect a Republican governor. As of 1994 that had not happened since the election of Don Samuelson in 1966. Even though he was pushing sixty-seven years old, Batt began his campaign with some strong headwinds. Confronted with three opponents in the GOP primary, Batt still won handily with almost 50 percent of the vote. In the general election, instead of facing John Peavey as expected, Batt would face Larry Echo Hawk, the incumbent state attorney general. Echo Hawk added a national component to the election since, if elected, he would be the first Native American governor in the country. The Echo Hawk campaign, because of its missteps and missed opportunities, has been seen as the worst in recent memory. The campaign miscues were visible, but the Republican organization may have been decisive.

Polls had Echo Hawk leading Batt by more than ten points throughout the campaign, and he received publicity (everywhere from the *New York*

Times to the *Times-Picayune* of New Orleans), money, and support (from celebrities such as Robert Redford and Dustin Hoffman) from throughout the country. Echo Hawk's membership in the Church of Latter-day Saints cut both ways in the state; he held a fundraiser on church property in Salt Lake City, but many members of the church still voted Republican. Ties to Bill Clinton, including billboard pictures of Echo Hawk and Clinton jogging, and a strong national Republican tide all worked in Batt's favor.

Through all of the noise, the party organization set up by Batt provided a clear advantage. Workers whom Batt had recruited for positions throughout the state paid back his loyalty with hours of volunteer support, fundraising, and organizational congruence. In 1994 and in subsequent elections the Republicans perfected the crucial tasks of voter education and get-out-the-vote measures, including absentee voting, through superior fundraising and utilizing the best practices of modern campaigning. Behind-the-scene workers, including Jeff Malman, Batt's campaign manager, would go on to use this experience to elect Republicans throughout the state for the next two decades. While the GOP was being propelled by its party strength, the Democratic organization was withering.

Successful Democratic campaigns in Idaho had been the result not of backing from an efficient party organization but the personal appeal of the candidate and the organizations supporting that candidacy. Frank Church and Cecil Andrus were the two most successful Democratic politicians in Idaho history. Each man won four statewide elections, while losing one. Ironically Andrus lost his first and Church lost his last. Both candidates were successful on their own, not relying on party organization and only indirectly helping other candidates in their party.

How could a Democratic senator who voted on the liberal side of most issues and was focused mostly on foreign affairs win so consistently in Idaho? Frank Church had one of the most acclaimed personal systems of constituency service. His Senate office was constantly in contact with voters to commemorate important events in constituents' lives. All letters and other communications were promptly answered. As the scholars Glenn Parker and Roger Davidson have noted, voters tend to love their member of Congress much more than Congress itself. While Congress as a whole is judged based on broad policy and on the pace of legislation, members of Congress are judged by service to constituents and personal characteristics.[7] In much the same manner Idahoans would vote for Church while panning the work of Congress.

Church had a loyal personal constituency. Many Idahoans would work and contribute to a Church campaign but would not work for the Idaho Democratic Party. Frank, along with his wife, Bethine, whose father and uncle were governors (the Clark brothers), had a wide circle of acquaintances who were personally loyal to the Churches and felt tied to Frank's success. This personal loyalty contributed to Frank Church's long string of electoral victories, but it did not translate into success for other Democratic candidates, especially when Church was not on the ballot.

Cecil Andrus came out of the woods of North Idaho to dominate state politics for much of the second half of the twentieth century. He was a loyal Democrat motivated by the call to service issued by John Kennedy in 1960.[8] Yet Andrus's campaigns and actions were focused not on party building but on electing Cecil Andrus. Much of Andrus's appeal was due to his larger-than-life personality. Whether it was having state troopers stop shipments of nuclear waste from entering Idaho or getting kicked by a mule, Cecil Andrus was the type of rugged individualist with whom most Idahoans identified. Hunting, fishing, using terms like "hornswoggling," or having his home phone number—there was no governor's mansion—listed in the phone book, Andrus the person was what caused people in Idaho to cast their ballots for him. They were not voting for Andrus the Democrat.

This analysis of Church and Andrus is not a criticism. If these men had relied on the Idaho Democratic organization, especially after the demise of Tom Boise, they would never have been so successful. In fact both Church and Andrus began their careers in opposition to Boise and his machine. In response, both Democrats created personal organizations in contrast to the party organization of Boise. This served them well but at the expense of the state Democratic Party.

DEMOGRAPHICS: UNIONS AND CALIFORNICATION

Idaho was settled initially by fur trappers, but soon it was miners and then loggers who dominated, at least in the northern part of the state. Miners and loggers would have a significant influence on the politics of the state until the 1990s, though their impact had begun to subside years earlier. While these extractive industries dominated by strong unions were on the decline, migration from other states changed the face of Idaho and the political landscape.

As in the rest of the country, labor unions flourished after World War II with the return of veterans and with the support of favorable legislation passed by Congress in the 1930s. Labor was a primary constituent of the Idaho Democratic Party, especially in North Idaho, and was often the difference in close races. Many a Democratic statewide victory was predicated on the late votes coming in from North Idaho, where timber and mining unions dominated the labor landscape. Providing election workers and money, unions were invaluable to Democrats and helped level the playing field against the natural Republican inclination of the state.

Labor membership declined across the entire country in the 1970s and 1980s, and Idaho was no different. Recession and economic contractions in the 1970s reduced the work force, especially in the extractive industries. Automation and environmental regulations from the national government further reduced the ranks of the timber and mining unions.

The turning point for the state was in 1985. In the 1950s right-to-work legislation had failed in the state legislature and on the ballot. Some Republicans believe the ballot measure in 1958 contributed to their loss of the majority in state legislature. In 1985 the state legislature finally passed right-to-work legislation—banning labor contracts that required membership in the union for employment—but the bill was vetoed by Democratic governor John Evans. The veto was overridden, and the law was upheld in a referendum the following year. The law created a cascade of job losses for unions and the end of Democratic dominance in North Idaho, which had become one of the more Jeffersonian and solidly Republican areas of the state. Without the workers, money, or votes from the timber and mining unions, only barely made up with inputs from civil service and teachers' unions, the Democratic Party lost the one group that could make the Democrats competitive outside of a few pockets (e.g., Boise, Sun Valley, Pocatello) throughout the state.

Idahoans for decades have complained about immigrants to the state from other parts of the country, with the most vitriol aimed at transplants from California. Seeing "Californication" as the bastardization of the state, Idahoans rue the increase of what many see as environmentalist, big-government liberals. The truth is the migrants from California have turned out to be more Jeffersonian and Republican than Idahoans themselves.

Who moves from California to Idaho? Although no systematic study has been performed, limited data show most new Idahoans from California come from Southern California. San Diego and Orange County are the dominant origins of the new inhabitants. With housing costs so much lower in Idaho, early retirees from California can upgrade their living accommodations dramatically with just the equity from their former homes. What types of Californians and to a lesser extent others have moved to Idaho in the last few decades? They tend to be disenchanted Californians. Tired of high taxes and intrusive government? Leave California and come to Idaho, the last frontier of freedom. Weary of the dominance of the Democratic Party in California for the last decades? Come to Idaho, where the Democrats are the endangered species.

Democrats have always had an uphill battle to win elections in Idaho. They had to work harder, raise more money, and get some Republicans to vote for their candidates. With the unions a shell of their former selves and more diehard Republicans moving to the state, the Democrats just can't will themselves to victory when the numbers are so stacked against them.

PETIT-IDEOLOGY: WHAT'S THE MATTER WITH IDAHO?

Organization and demographics can explain only part of the success of the Republican Party in Idaho. Attachment to party runs deeper than a few variables. How well a political party can mesh its position with the dominant views of the electorate can foretell success in elections for decades to come. How the Republican Party in Idaho, and to some extent the party nationwide, was able to synchronize its principles with those of the voters has been described for other states and nationally. Some of this understanding can be applied to Idaho.

After the 1930s the positions of the two political parties in the United States began to diverge on the petit-ideology spectrum. Initially each party generally adhered to one side of the spectrum. The Democrats were the Jeffersonians in policy areas pushing for limited government and the preeminence of the individual. The Republicans, as the descendants of the Federalists and Whigs, were the Hamiltonians in policy areas supporting an energetic government to boost the economy and promote the general

will of the public. Franklin Roosevelt and the New Deal began the splinter-
ing of the parties' traditional allegiances along the petit-ideology spectrum.

In response to the Great Depression, Democrats began to support government involvement in the economy. FDR and Democrats who followed
him believed that individuals could not fend for themselves without assistance from the government. The collective good in the economic realm was
too important and precarious to leave to the workings of the marketplace.
Thus on economic issues the Democrats had become Hamiltonians. Some
of these views slid over into the area of social issues, but a clear fissure
was visible decades later.

As the twentieth century progressed, the Democrats, especially after the
civil rights movement, reverted to a Jeffersonian position on social issues,
including racial matters. Abortion and women's issues in the 1970s showed
the extent of the party's shift to inconsistent positions on the petit-ideology
spectrum. The party advocated for the individual over government and
society on noneconomic issues. This approach by the national party would
have significant ramifications for the Democratic Party in Idaho.

While the Democratic Party was developing a split personality in regard
to petit-ideology, so were the Republicans. Although the corporate faction
of the Republicans did not favor excessive government involvement in
economic affairs, after the rush of the New Deal slowed they were comfortable with government mechanisms to fine-tune the economy. Among
Republicans there was little or no opposition to social welfare programs of
the national government during the Eisenhower administration. This pas-
sive stance began to change in the 1960s with the rise of neoconservatism.

With William F. Buckley as their intellectual muse, the neoconservatives
sought a return to the Jeffersonian vision of political economy. Barry Goldwater was the vanguard and Ronald Reagan eventually ascended to lead
the movement of these Jeffersonians who wished to return the individual
to preeminence in the economy, with as little government involvement as
possible.[9] This approach led to a conflict in the social policy arena during
the same time the Democrats were trumpeting Jeffersonian approaches
to social policy.

The Republicans of the 1980s began to believe in a more authority-
based rather than individual approach on social issues. With the rise of
the so-called Christian Coalition and other faith-based pressure groups,

the Republicans began to support government intervention into issues that revolved around abortion, women's rights, and religious issues. A schism along the petit-ideology spectrum was forming in both parties.

This is a rough examination of the situation. There were issues on which the parties did not fit perfectly into this typology. Democrats sought governmental solutions on civil rights issues in a Hamiltonian approach. Republicans were Jeffersonian in their views on gun control. Not all members or even elected officials assiduously toed the line on these matters. As the 1990s approached, Republicans were generally becoming more Jeffersonian on economic issues but Hamiltonian on social issues, while the Democrats were more likely to be Hamiltonian on economic issues and Jeffersonian on social issues.

How or why this inconsistency within the parties developed is not clear. Historians such as Rick Perlstein have seen the Republican emphasis on social issues as a calculated electoral maneuver aimed at winning votes from those seeking more "order" in society. Perlstein's books on Nixon and Reagan see the focus of Republicans on social and racial components of public policy as a calculated move by the party to drive a wedge between factions within the Democratic Party often seen as the New Deal coalition. If Republicans could get white southerners and blue-collar workers to concentrate on social issues instead of their own economic welfare, then Republicans could win them over to their side regardless of the popularity of government programs such as Medicare.[10]

Thomas Frank looks at the situation in a similar manner in his study *What's the Matter with Kansas?*[11] In an 1896 essay with the same title William Allen White attacked the populists and defended the Republicans and presidential candidate William McKinley. Frank takes the opposite approach, asking why voters in Kansas who tend to be poor farmers and blue-collar workers vote for Republicans who support economic policies that primarily benefit wealthy financiers. In virulent terms that hearken back to the orator William Jennings Bryan and show his contempt for the Republican Party, Frank describes the "Great Backlash," which is strikingly similar to Perlstein's thesis. Frank argues that Republicans were attempting to lure voters by reminding them that Democrats had bused children to distant schools to achieve racial integration and had supported exhibits featuring un-Christian or blasphemous art. He concludes that Republicans were attempting to steal the hearts and minds of these former populists in Kansas so that the GOP could implement economic policies that punish the poor and reward the rich. Frank's anti-Republican mission is clear, but hiding behind his vitriol is some truth that can be useful in understanding the fall of the Idaho Democratic Party.

The Republicans in Idaho, with assistance from the national party, were able to emphasize social issues from the Hamiltonian perspective while downplaying economic issues that might favor the Democrats. As Ronald Reagan, Jerry Falwell, and Pat Robertson pushed morality encouraged by the government on the national level, their protégés in Idaho helped make the Republican Party almost invincible electorally. Women seemed to be the best standard-bearers for this Hamiltonian social message. Beginning with Helen Chenoweth and continuing through Anne Fox and eventually Sherri Ybarra, Republican candidates were seen as upholding the morality of society.

Democrats seemed to add fuel to the fire. In Idaho they tried to campaign as down-to-earth commoners, but national Democrats, especially presidential contenders, kept stepping on the Idaho Democrats' message. Whether it was Jimmy Carter, Bill Clinton, John Kerry, Barack Obama, or House Speaker Nancy Pelosi voicing messages seen as elitist, Democratic candidates in Idaho had to compete against Republicans in their own state and against Democrats on the national level. In statewide races the Democrats tried running "moderate" candidates such as John Peavey and Keith Allred, both of whom were ranchers, but they could never get past the taint of the Democrats in Washington DC. As in the Kansas case, even though Democrats supported issues that should have been popular with Idahoans due to their economic situation, voters in the state felt the strong Hamiltonian pull of government using its power and authority to promote a morally sound society.

IS THERE ANYTHING WRONG WITH IDAHO?

Idahoans, like most Americans, are at odds with themselves in terms of the petit-ideology spectrum. Many tend to be Jeffersonian on economic issues and Hamiltonian on social issues. Although having an inconsistent belief system has been the norm in the country for decades, though sometimes in the opposite manner, the Republican Party has functioned well when people's beliefs run in these dual paths. Along with a stronger organization and favorable demographics, the Idaho Republican Party has been dominant for more than two decades.

So are Idaho Democrats destined to go the way of the Whigs? Well, the party has not done much to reverse its fortunes. Obviously a more effective organization that uses modern forms of analytics and sophisticated voter outreach would be helpful. Demographics could actually be moving in the direction of the Democrats, given a surging Hispanic population that leans Democratic and will be coming of age. Organization could greatly enhance the potential impact of this demographic change.

Petit-ideology and the strained relationship between the national party and the Idaho Democrats is a much more obtuse dilemma for the latter. Presidential candidates who are out of touch with "Idaho values" provide a persistent headwind to any candidate running as a Democrat in Idaho. That said, relying on the party has never been a means for Democrats to get elected in Idaho. If future candidates follow the game plan of Frank Church or Cecil Andrus, they would build their own organization, ignore the national Democrats, and synchronize their petit-ideology with that of the voters of the state. Idaho may never become a "blue" state, but with some work and some luck it could perhaps turn "purple."

The political parties in Idaho have been far from competitive in recent years. The Democratic Party in Idaho has not provided voters with a viable alternative to the dominant Republicans. The competition in Idaho is not between the political parties but between the two poles of petit-ideology within the Republican Party. The libertarian Jeffersonians battle against the communitarian Hamiltonians within the Republican primaries, while general elections are a foregone conclusion. While most states and the nation as a whole may be understood by examining the conflict between the parties, that partisanship does not explain conflict within a one-party state such as Idaho. Petit-ideology fills the void in explaining the political environment in Idaho.

CHAPTER TEN

Intergovernmental Relations

A CLEAR EXAMPLE OF MILES'S LAW

How should different levels or branches of government interact with each other? Are decisions best made at one level or branch of government or another? Where should power be lodged? Which powers should be lodged where? Such questions are endemic in any federal system of government. There are no simple answers to these questions, though the different poles of petit-ideology provide some answers. It seems one's views on power and its distribution depend on one's position in the power structure.

THREE MANNERS OF INTERGOVERNMENTAL RELATIONS

Interactions between different parts of government are the realm of public administration studies. Typically when we use the term "intergovern-mental," the meaning applies to various levels of government, as if the levels were different systems. However, if we look at the American federal system of government, each level is an integral part of the same system. The separate branches of government that occupy the same level are also parts of the same system and have intertwining relationships with each other. The three types of relationships, between each of three levels and between branches, are critical for understanding state government. State government's relationships with the national government, local govern-ment, and among the different branches of the state government provide insight into the essence of the various parts of the government.

The relationship between a semi-autonomous state government, such as Idaho, and the national government is typically referred to as federalism.[1]

A thorough examination of federalism is beyond the scope of this work and not necessary for the analysis that follows.[2] A survey of how federalism has been interpreted throughout American history is necessary for the purposes of what follows.

For most of the history of the country the relationship between the national government and the states could be described as dual federalism. There was a clear delineation between the powers of the national government and the powers of the states. Where did that dividing line of power lie? Under this interpretation of federalism, the national government had only the powers granted to it in the Constitution, with the remaining inherent powers of government being reserved to the states. This view was most clearly articulated in the Tenth Amendment to the Constitution. This interpretation was dominant from the ratification of the Constitution until it was set aside by the Supreme Court in 1937.

Although some could argue the Civil War ended the prevalence of the dual federalism interpretation, actions by the Supreme Court in the twentieth century, including the *Lockner* decision and rulings against the National Recovery Act and the Agricultural Adjustment Administration, still supported this limited view of the extent of the national government's powers. Cases in 1937 upholding the National Labor Relations Act and other portions of the New Deal signaled the end of dual federalism as the paradigm of federalism, thus yielding to a more amorphous understanding of the national-state relationship.

Through the rest of the twentieth century, the national government and the states shared responsibilities and powers, and the federalism of that era could be referred to as cooperative federalism. Powers were not strictly segregated between the two levels of government; certain substantive policy areas were instead administered jointly, if not exactly equally, by both the states and the national government. Policies concerning poverty, transportation, and education, including the No Child Left Behind Act of 2001, were financed to a greater extent by the national government, which gave it greater influence over areas under the purview of the states than under the doctrine of dual federalism. Although this iteration is called "cooperative" federalism, because the national government began providing greater amounts of funding for particular services, the power of the states waned.

Although not superseding cooperative federalism, an interpretation of federalism that can be termed creative or regulated federalism had become prevalent by 1964. Instead of sharing responsibilities in policy areas, creative federalism saw the national government creating policies and imposing them on the states. The rationale was that certain policies (e.g., civil rights and the environment) needed to be consistent and uniform across the country.

The relationship between a state government and the local governments within its territory is vastly different from the federal relationship between the national government and the states. While states are semi-autonomous and have certain inherent or reserved powers, local governments are merely creatures of the states. This view of the subservient relationship of local governments was most famously promulgated by John Forrest Dillon. Dillon's Rule, as it came to be known, is best elucidated through the judge's own words in his opinion in *Clinton v. Cedar Rapids and the Missouri River Railroad*, handed down when he was on the Iowa supreme court: "Municipal corporations owe their origin to, and derive their powers and rights wholly from, the legislature. It breathes into them the breath of life, without which they cannot exist. As it creates, so may it destroy. If it may destroy, it may abridge and control."[3]

The structure, jurisdiction, and powers of local governments are specifically determined by the state. This applies to all types of local governments: city, county, school, or any variety of special district. This relationship is not balanced at all and even pales in relation to the most egregious forms of cooperative or creative federalism.

The relationship among the three branches of government on the state level is very similar to what most people have understood to exist on the national level. The understanding may be cogent even though the term typically used for the relationship is at best misleading.

The relationship among legislative, executive, and judiciary branches is stereotypically described as "separation of powers." Although it is used in every situation and form, the term is faulty. A more accurate phrase would be "separated institutions sharing powers."[4] The branches cannot act on their own: the powers are not separate; the branches are separate.

The legislature cannot pass laws without the governor being involved, either positively or negatively. The executive branch is needed to enforce the laws. The courts are also involved in ensuring there is fair execution of the law. The appointment process includes the governor and the state senate. These examples show how the relations among the branches are not simply branches exercising powers in isolation; institutions must work together to act in a positive manner.

"WHERE YOU STAND DEPENDS ON WHERE YOU SIT"

Miles's Law simply states that "where you stand depends on where you sit." Developed by a government analyst named Rufus E. Miles Jr. to explain the changing beliefs of individuals after they have switched positions in the government bureaucracy, the essence of the theory is apparent in other situations as well.[5] Individuals in positions at different levels of government would seem to look at the world from a different perspective and have different beliefs about how government should function in their own circle of the governmental world. A bureaucrat or elected official serving in the national government will look at a situation differently than would someone in state government. That same state official will have a different perception of the particular event or condition than a local government official would have. The handling of a particular circumstance is based on one's perspective. Miles's Law attempts to explain the changes of behavior that result in changes in the actor's position.

WHY MILES'S LAW? INSTITUTIONAL RATIONAL CHOICE

How does one explain the changes in behavior described by Miles's Law? Are these people hypocrites? Are they irrational? This phenomenon could be chalked up merely to the vagaries of rational individuals looking out for their own preferences and best interests. Others posit that changes in stated opinions are mere hypocrisy, with one of the positions being the person's true feelings and the other being a false front. Miles does not see such changes in these terms. It is a change in perspective that changes positions. Institutions, and one's place within the institution, matter. Changing institutions change one's perspective and, in turn, how one looks at the world. It seems simple but flies in the face of the belief in the personal constancy of petit-ideology.

By the 1980s political scientists were wrestling with the questions of trying to reconcile anomalies within rational choice theory. Progress was made when theorists took the rational actor out of a hermetically sealed world with no extraneous factors and placed the actor within the world of institutions. The predictive construct that combined institutionalism with rational choice theory came to be known as institutional rational choice (IRC).[6]

IRC begins with the rational actor who has preferences, as well as beliefs on how specific actions will achieve those preferences, and then chooses actions, again based on those beliefs, that will most efficiently achieve his or her preferences. Institutional arrangements are the rules within institutions that circumscribe actions by the individual actor. Actors assume roles within the institution based on their position and the rules that govern the particular actor. Different actors who see themselves in different roles will choose different actions, not because the actors are different but because the institutional arrangements the actors face are different. It is the institution, or more specifically the institutional arrangements, that influence behavior.

Institutions circumscribe behavior. They provide the boundaries, partitions, and framework for behavior.[7] If potential behavior can be viewed as an open field, then institutions can be thought of as hedges, moats, and fences that constrain, inhibit, and channel action into defined areas. Another analogy for institutions and their importance and effect can be seen in sports. A football game without rules turns into a mass of competing humanity with no structure or form. Institutions prescribe the boundaries of the field, the number of players on each side, what plays or actions are permitted, what penalties are assessed for infractions, who decides when an infraction has occurred, when the game is eventually over, and who has triumphed. The action of the players will change as the rules of the game are changed. Their rationality is fixed. It is the institution, when changed, that will determine the actions of the players.

Miles's Law is basically a simplified version of institutional rational choice theory. When one changes seats, so to speak, it is actually an actor moving from one institution to another. IRC would posit that changing seats would change the actor's behavior. Before moving on to an example, it is imperative to look first at the two poles, or seats, of petit-ideology as they pertain to intergovernmental relations.

PETIT-IDEOLOGY AND INTERGOVERNMENTAL RELATIONS

From the nation's beginning Hamilton wanted the national government to have greater authority than the states. According to one scholar, "fear of the power of states was the primary driving force behind Hamilton's efforts to strengthen national government."[8] Another notes that "Hamilton was an ultranationalist."[9] During the Revolutionary War, Hamilton, writing under the pseudonym "The Continentalist," pointed to the need for strength within the national government and especially to the need to "ENLARGE THE POWERS OF CONGRESS."[10] He saw the inability of the Continental Congress to lead the nation and the lack of fortitude by the states in executing the war, especially in the area of funding, as reasons to be pessimistic about the cause of independence.

This preference for the power of a central national government over the divided power of individual states becomes even more prevalent when changes to the Articles of Confederation were proposed and the Constitution was being ratified. In his famous June 18, 1787, speech to the Constitutional Convention, Hamilton argues, "The general power whatever be its form if it preserves itself, must swallow up the State powers, otherwise it will be swallowed up by them. . . . Two Sovereignties can not co-exist with the same limits."[11] Hamilton saw the Constitution as an improvement over the Articles, but it still "left the national government with much less power than Hamilton considered necessary."[12] Hamilton begins *Federalist Paper* No. 7 with his critique of how the constant squabbling among the states could be stemmed only with a robust national government. Through later essays Hamilton espoused how a more robust central government, implicitly at the expense of the states, would assist the nation in commerce and revenues. The lack of trade and wealth were minor concerns to Hamilton compared to the military weakness of the national government, a weakness made manifest by Shays's Rebellion. Due to the large expanse of the new country, Hamilton contended that only a mighty central government could govern it.

Governmental power is sometimes reduced to two aspects: the ability to raise revenue and the ability to wage war. Through his defense of the Constitution, Hamilton indicated that the only way for the nation to be successful would be to wrest these powers from the states and lodge them in the new, expansive national government created by the Constitution.

As secretary of the treasury, Alexander Hamilton worked steadily to increase the power and influence of the national government, usually at the expense of the states. In his *Report on Manufactures* Hamilton proposes the use of mercantile policies, if even only temporarily, to increase the production capacity of the country. The national government would thus be called on to actively promote industry. There was no thought that any other level of government could assume such a role.

Hamilton supported the national government in the realm of finance and currency to an even greater degree. His promotion of the Bank of the United States, desire for robust tax collections, and, most prominently, the national government's assumption of the states' Revolutionary War debt were all policies that Hamilton believed would strengthen the national government vis-à-vis the states. Having bondholders beholden to the national government instead of the states would make the financial class, whom Hamilton felt were truly the core of the nation, pledge their allegiance to the central government, which would further sap the strength of the weaker states.

Hamilton's belief in the need for a national government whose powers were greater than those of the states was consistent and constant. As one scholar notes, "Through the patronage that coursed downward, multiple dependencies would result, reducing individual independence and, in Hamilton's judgment, acting as a safeguard against disorder."[13] Furthermore, "Hamilton was absorbed with establishing a sovereign and powerful national government capable of protecting the national interest."[14] This approach was directly in opposition to Jefferson's faith in the virtue of the individual and state governments.

As suggested earlier during the discussion of the branches of state government, Hamilton was an advocate for the preeminence of the executive and judiciary branches at the expense of the legislative branch. His views on the balance between the legislature and executive were formulated during his time in the Continental Army and because of his experiences with the ineptitude of the Continental Congress in trying to lead the military effort without an executive. His views on the subject during the Constitutional Convention leaned toward an elected monarchy, which he believed would assure the independence and power of the executive. In his defense of the Constitution during the ratification debate Hamilton chided those fearful of a single executive and instead exalted the need for a forceful president. He noted in *Federalist Paper* No. 70, "Energy in the Executive is a leading character in the definition of good government."[15] His support for a vigorous and independent judiciary was no less fervent.

In Hamilton's view the judiciary was both the most important guardian of minority rights and a bulwark against the majoritarian tendencies of the legislature. To this end Hamilton, in *Federalist Paper* No. 78, makes the argument for the judiciary to have the power to strike down laws passed by Congress that are contrary to the Constitution. The concept of judicial review was not widely shared by the other participants at the convention, but with the passage of time and with support from Chief Justice John Marshall the ability of courts to rule legislative and executive actions void is now seen as natural and an important aspect of the relationship among the branches.

Thomas Jefferson's belief in the nobility of the common farmer extended to state and local government, which in his time was dominated by individuals of this ilk. Government closer to the people was seen as more responsive to the "common" people and more accountable to the public than a consolidated national government with a capital far removed from most citizens.

Jefferson's views have been further articulated, refined, and given an academic gloss by public choice theorists.[16] How is local government more responsive and accountable? According to public choice theory, if one is unhappy with a policy of the local government, it is rational and efficient to move one's residency to a better place. If the national government has an objectionable policy, "voting with one's feet" becomes much more difficult. This economically based theory is a long way from Jefferson's thoughts but shows how the basic premise is still a powerful force in the country, at least among scholars.

Jefferson was not present or even in the country during the writing of or the debates on the Constitution. His writings never explicitly state that he was against the Constitution—though he desired a bill of rights. His statements do indicate that he thought the national government needed additional power over commerce, but to a more limited extent than what was ultimately ratified. Jefferson did have concerns with the convention itself and with his friend James Madison's involvement. It seems Jefferson's concerns about the Constitution were more focused on the forces behind the convention than on the product of the convention itself.[17]

After Hamilton was able to create a financial structure of national import, Jefferson began to reveal more of his beliefs on the need for providing more power to the states. Jefferson's proposals for a shift of power from the national government to the states reached a crescendo after the passage of the Alien and Sedition Acts during John Adams's presidency. With the aid of Madison, Jefferson developed the doctrine of state interposition, which is more commonly referred to as nullification. Jefferson did not think officials of the national government, whether the president or judges, could objectively determine the limits of the power of the national government. Instead each state would be able on its own to determine whether federal authorities within the particular state had exercised powers not given the national government by the Constitution. In essence each state could declare actions by the national government "null and void" within the state. Eventually the idea of nullification would become the basis of resolutions passed by legislatures in Kentucky and Virginia, but such ideas did not receive support beyond these states until South Carolina launched its dispute with Pres. Andrew Jackson over tariffs.[18]

Jefferson, in opposition to Hamilton, felt that the legislature should be the preeminent branch relative to any other level of government. His qualms concerning the Constitution in this regard included his fear that the House of Representatives was inadequate and that the president would be elected for life. He felt that Congress should have the power to override opinions of the courts similar to the way the president could veto legislation passed by Congress.[19] With the legislature being closest to the people, Jefferson felt Congress should determine policy and that the other branches should have only limited roles in making policy.

BUTCH OTTER: A JEFFERSONIAN WHO CHANGED SEATS

Testing the plausibility of either IRC or Miles's Law is beyond the scope of this project. A thorough examination of a large number of cases would be needed in order to do so. Choosing one specific case won't disprove a theory or "law," but using a properly chosen case study can enlighten researchers on the relevant factors to be studied. Examining an Idaho politician who has served in many positions or seats can help illuminate the relevance of Miles's Law to petit-ideology and Idaho politics.

C. L. "Butch" Otter started his electoral career in 1972 after graduating from the College of Idaho. Political success for Otter was no accident. According to one observer, "He was the most gifted Idaho campaigner in the second half of [the twentieth] century, a great salesman, full of charm, perpetually bubbling over, almost impossible to dislike."[20] Although lumped together with others under the amorphous label of "conservative," Otter was truly a Jeffersonian carved out of libertarian Canyon County fresh on the heels of Steve Symms.

Otter's Jeffersonian credentials were established when he did not support what was considered antipornography legislation (reportedly stating, "I don't vote 'no,' I vote 'hell no'"). He did not see that legislation or the government as the solution for a social ill. Otter's short stint in the state legislature, just two terms, showed an independent streak that tacked closely to the Jeffersonian pole of petit-ideology.

After losing a bid for governor in 1978, Otter stayed out of politics and worked in the private sector until 1986, when he was elected lieutenant governor, a post he would be elected to four times. He would serve as lieutenant governor longer than anyone else in Idaho history. The lieutenant governor, as mentioned earlier, has little to do unless the governor is out of the state, and then the lieutenant governor fills in as governor. On one such occasion Otter showed his Jeffersonian side again. The state legislature had passed a law to raise the drinking age in Idaho to twenty-one, since Congress had passed a law withholding highway funds from any state that did not have a drinking age of twenty-one. Otter, sitting in for Governor Andrus, who was traveling out of state, vetoed the bill. Otter's action had little impact, however, because Andrus signed a second bill upon his return.

After fourteen years as lieutenant governor, Otter ran for Congress and was elected from the First Congressional District of Idaho in 2000. He would serve in the U.S. House of Representatives for three terms. As in the state legislature, Otter voted most often with his party. One issue on which he strayed from party lines was in regard to the USA PATRIOT Act in 2001, when Otter joined just two other Republicans in opposing the legislation. Otter continued through his tenure in Congress to oppose government surveillance powers. His vote on the landmark 2001 bill was seen as a defining act of Otter's career.[21] Of course these votes and subsequent statements did not affect the policies.

After three terms in the U.S. House, Otter ran for governor again in 2006, but this time he won easily. Otter would be elected governor of Idaho for three consecutive terms. As governor, Butch Otter still spoke out against the national government and in favor of limited government overall. In keeping with Miles's Law he made decisions that were more Hamiltonian in nature and were in contrast to the views of more strident Jeffersonians in the state legislature.

In 2009 Governor Otter proposed increasing the state gasoline tax by seven cents to address a lack of highway funding. Tax increases of any kind are anathema to a Jeffersonian of Otter's ilk, even if the tax would be for highway funding, which many would see as the proper role of state government. Otter went so far as to veto a number of appropriations bills during the session in an attempt to persuade the legislature to pass his gasoline tax. In the end Otter could not get the state legislators to support his policy of more government taxation and spending.

After the passage of the Affordable Care Act in 2010, each state had the option of setting up its own state health-care exchange or standing aside and letting state residents buy medical insurance on the national exchange. Many Idaho politicians who leaned toward the Jeffersonian view of antipathy toward the national government wanted to have nothing to do with "Obamacare." Otter, though an explicit opponent of Obama's health-care plan, supported it and convinced the state legislature to set up a state insurance exchange. Pragmatism overwhelmed ideology for the Jeffersonian sitting in the governor's chair.

JEFFERSON, OTTER, AND MILES

Had Otter lost his way in forty years, as he went from the firebrand Jeffersonian in the state house to a compromising conciliator as a governor? Was he betraying the views of Jefferson or had he merely learned to be a "statesman"? Or was Otter following Miles's Law?

The "learning" hypothesis is what Otter himself proposed in the wake of his 2009 proposal to raise the state gasoline tax and subsequent vetoes to goad the legislature to follow his lead. Governor Otter claimed he had learned a great deal since he was state Representative Otter in the legislature. Quoting a former Speaker of the Idaho house of representatives, Otter noted that ideology can assist in setting goals but that "in order to get to those goals, you're gonna have to act pragmatically."[22]

The Miles's Law hypothesis was also proposed during the 2009 gasoline tax fight. Randy Stapilus, a preeminent observer of Idaho politics, at the time contended that Otter had not changed as much as the times and his position had changed. "Over the stretch of three decades, a few things change," Stapilus said. "For one thing, Butch is not in a position now to declaim an ideology or a stance and leave it at that—he actually has to govern."[23] Sitting in the governor's chair can change one's stand on the issues.

Is Otter that different from others? Even Thomas Jefferson, whose views characterize one pole of petit-ideology, could be pragmatic when sitting in the president's chair. When France offered to sell the United States all of the Louisiana Territory at pennies an acre, Jefferson's first reaction was that the president, according to the Constitution, could not approve such a purchase. In broad terms Jefferson did not believe the national government had the power to purchase land without amending the Constitution. Convinced that waiting for the tedious amendment process of proposal and ratification would allow France to back out of the deal, Jefferson swallowed his misgivings and persuaded the Congress to approve the deal. The benefits of the deal, which included the acquisition of land that could support Jefferson's vision of an agrarian nation for centuries to come, outweighed the ideological qualms he had about the deal.

Miles's Law in the examples noted here shows that changing seats can change where a person stands on the spectrum of petit-ideology. Although more examples and more precise methodological techniques are needed to make concrete claims, it seems that Jeffersonians, when sitting in an executive's chair, become more like the pragmatic Wilsonians. When one has to govern, it is better to act like Wilson than either Jefferson or Hamilton. Again, as in other areas of Idaho's governmental structure and political environment, petit-ideology provides a useful method for understanding political behavior.

Epilogue

CHILD SUPPORT, SHARIA LAW, AND CULTURE CLASH

On April 29, 2015, Gov. C. L. "Butch" Otter issued a proclamation calling the Idaho state legislature into an extraordinary (or special) session on May 18, 2015. The session was to be limited to considering legislation that would bring Idaho into conformity with an international treaty negotiated and ratified by the national government.

The circumstances around this special session can most clearly be understood through the prism of petit-ideology. Following a short description of the background of this situation, the event is examined by exploring the positions of the main players along the spectrum of petit-ideology. This example confirms how petit-ideology can be a valuable tool in political analysis.

IDAHO AND AN INTERNATIONAL TREATY

In 2007 the United States signed The Hague Convention on the International Recovery of Child Support and Other Forms of Family Maintenance. The stated purpose of the treaty was to make it easier to track delinquent parents in countries throughout the world. All fifty states had to rewrite their regulations in order for the treaty to go into effect in the United States, as child support is administered jointly by the states and national government. As of April 2015 nineteen states had passed the necessary regulations, with no states rejecting outright the addition of the new language to their laws.

The Idaho state legislature took up the issue at the end of its 2015 session. The state senate passed the new regulations proposed by the state Department of Health and Welfare on a voice vote with no dissent. On the last day of the session the bill was taken up by the Judiciary Committee in the lower chamber of the legislature. The committee tabled the bill on a 9-to-8 vote, effectively killing the measure for the session.

The timeliness of the bill was made clear after the state legislature adjourned sine die. Without the passage of these amended regulations, Idaho was facing the loss of $16 million in federal funds (two-thirds of its child support enforcement budget) and all access to the federal system that enforced an annual total of $205 million in child support payments to Idaho. An additional sum of $30 million in federal assistance to needy Idaho families was also in jeopardy.[1]

Those opposed to the legislation held a number of objections. Rep. Kim Simms argued that the bill would undermine Idaho sovereignty. She felt that the state would have to enforce child support agreements created in other nations. This led to the view, expressed by Sen. Sheryl Nuxoll, that Idaho would have to enforce child support laws adjudicated from countries under Sharia Law, the legal system derived from the religious precepts of Islam. Rep. Lynn Luker claimed approval of the treaty provisions would open up databases controlled by the national government and allow foreign countries to gain access to personal information from those databases. Some people, both legislators and members of the public, believed that the national government was coercing, or blackmailing, the state into action the state would otherwise not take. This argument is related to that raised by Representative Simms concerning state sovereignty.

Those who supported the legislation, including many interest groups, the governor, and legislative leaders, argued that the loss of funds and access to the national database were not worth the benefits of making a statement on state sovereignty. It was estimated that more than 150,000 children living in Idaho would be adversely affected if the state did not enact the regulations. The governor noted it was "deadbeat parents" that supporters of the regulations were after.[2]

The special session began on May 18, 2015, after the governor and legislative leaders had crafted an amended bill to include changes that satisfied some opponents without altering the basic aspects of the legislation. The

Ways and Means Committee voted to introduce the bill and send it to a joint meeting of the house and senate Judiciary Committees for a public hearing. The house's Judiciary Committee, after an extended and vigorous debate, sent the bill to the floor on a 12-to-5 vote. The Idaho house, after more debate, passed the bill on a 49-to-21 vote. After a unanimous vote by the senate's Judiciary Committee to send the bill to the senate floor, the entire Idaho senate voted 33-to-2 in favor of the legislation. The entire session last under twelve hours. Governor Otter signed the bill into law the following day.[3]

EXAMINING IDAHO USING PETIT-IDEOLOGY

Much like the example of the ultrasound legislation from the introduction, the Idaho state government's reactions and actions concerning the international treaty on child support are best understood through the prism of petit-ideology. More common typologies such as liberal versus conservative or Democrat versus Republican do not clearly demarcate the divisions created on this issue. Petit-ideology may not be sufficient for the examination of all political issues, but it is very illuminating when we attempt to understand the political divisions in Idaho and possibly the rest of the country.

The Jeffersonian pole of petit-ideology supports the individual's right to liberty and freedom of action. Society is a collection of individuals and not an entity unto itself. The views of the majority are held in the highest esteem, especially compared to the positions of the elite. The role of government should be strictly circumscribed and concentrated on the protection of individual property rights. When government action is required, the level of government closest to the people is preferred. The opponents of the child support law tended to tack toward this Jeffersonian view.

The opponents of the child support bill voiced their greatest opposition to the dominance of the national government over the state of Idaho. Arguments concerning losing state sovereignty and being blackmailed or coerced by the national government were clearly Jeffersonian in character. In their view state government is closer to the people and should be the power base from which individuals may express their opinions and preferences. The national government, especially with regard to an international treaty, in their view is unconcerned with the individual and wants to impose elitist, international norms on the people of Idaho. Even Representative Luker's argument on the loss of privacy for child support records fits within the Jeffersonian framework. The private information of individuals should be protected even if it is to be used to provide assistance in collecting support from "deadbeat" parents.

The Hamiltonian pole of petit-ideology focuses on the welfare of the community as a whole, at the expense of the individual. In this view the common good should be the aim of both society and the individuals who make up that society. The entire collection of individuals in society may not, however, have the ability to discern the common good. Those with specialized knowledge may be needed to show society the best path for the collective. With society as a whole being the focus, government provides a necessary function in helping to achieve the goals of the community. The larger national government should be preferred over state and local governments, as it is more detached from the pettiness and parochialism of individuals. The executive and judiciary branches are preferred over the legislature, as they too will be more detached from the people and more able to discern and act in the interests of the whole, rather than the various parts of society.

Supporters of the bill to bring Idaho law into conformity with the international treaty were Hamiltonian in their outlook. They saw the need for the national government to work with other governments in order to assure timely payments to children and their custodians. The community would be hurt without the money for dependents and without access to the database to collect the payments. Society, through government, was seen as the answer to individuals who did not fulfill their responsibilities. It was in the individual self-interest of noncustodial parents to renege on their obligations to their children even though such actions could be seen as detrimental to society. Even the use of the term "deadbeat" is a means of shaming the individual for not living up to the ideals of society.

This petit-ideology split among Idahoans, and especially the Republican Party of Idaho, was evident even to the media. When the controversy first started, the *Boise Weekly* recognized the division between the Jeffersonians and Hamiltonians. Siding with the Jeffersonian view was Representative Luker, as noted earlier. In response to Luker, other Republicans aligned with Hamilton saw the issue differently. Rep. Luke Malek exclaimed, "I do not support the erratic behavior that will lead to the dismantling of our child support system, nor the implication that this mockery of a legal analysis in any way represents our Republican caucus."[4]

The fight between Jeffersonians and Hamiltonians went beyond simple party conflict. Representative Malek wrote a couple of editorials, the first attacking those who did not favor the child support bill. In one he wrote that "the decision to deconstruct child-support enforcement in Idaho was an erratic decision made by nine people in the legislature. They have violated Republican principles by turning their backs on fiscal, economic and legal stability. Perhaps it was the thrill of using this bill to make a statement."[5] A subsequent editorial had Malek confronting the Idaho Freedom Foundation, the most Jeffersonian interest group in the state. Wayne Hoffman, the head of that foundation, responded in icy and vitriolic terms.[6] Petit-ideology was the true dividing line in this confrontation over child support.

Why does this issue, like many others, fall along the spectrum of petit-ideology? Why do people tend to rely on the values of one pole or the other when making determinations on issues? Petit-ideology can be thought of as a heuristic, a time-saving device. When confronted with a new and unique situation, people have a tendency to fall back on established beliefs rather than comprehensively determining the costs and benefits presented in each situation that arises. The legislators and other Idahoans were presented with a very complex international treaty on child support and had to decide how to react. The default position was to fall back on the petit-ideology position that had served them well in the past. The Jeffersonians saw this treaty as an incursion, as coercion by the centralized national government to force the state government to bow to its wishes at the expense of the freedom and personal property (i.e., information) of the individuals of the state. The Hamiltonians saw the law as a means to ensure that selfish individuals (i.e., "deadbeats") live up to their responsibilities to the community. The national government had, through its constitutional powers, negotiated a treaty that would help society deal with the issue of children living with only one parent.

This is not to say that parents who did not pay their court-ordered child support were lazy or evil. This is just how human minds work. People have to make sense of a complicated world despite incomplete knowledge and limited cognitive ability. Shortcuts are necessary and often beneficial. Our intuition and "gut feelings" are often more effective than attempts at rational analysis.[7] Petit-ideology is just an explanation of how people react to their world.

Using petit-ideology to assist in understanding the political world seems convenient while also being effective. Readers need to decide for themselves whether it is applicable to a specific situation or individual action. Social science certainly needs another item in its toolbox for understanding individuals and society as a whole.

Petit-ideology does not seem to be limited to Idaho. Strains of the conflict between visions of the individual versus the community are reflected in policy disputes in other areas of the country and in the nation as a whole. One could argue that the current divisions in the national Republican Party are a result of conflicts along the petit-ideology spectrum.

So, are we done? Far from it. These examples in one state provide but a sampling of the relevant evidence for the effectiveness of a new theory. The work has just begun. Petit-ideology needs to be tested in other circumstances, other environments, and other contexts. That is much beyond the scope of this meager exercise. This new tool should be taken out of the box to see whether it could be useful in situations beyond those covered in this book. Now that the theory has been built, it needs to be taken out for a spin. With respect to the inadequacies of current social science methodologies, petit-ideology seems to be worth a try.

NOTES

INTRODUCTION

1. Legislature of the State of Idaho, Senate Bill No. 1387.
2. Betsy Z. Russell, "Bill Would Require Ultrasound for Abortion," *Spokesman Review* (Spokane WA), February 28, 2012, 1A.
3. Quoted in Russell, "Bill Would Require Ultrasound for Abortion," 1A.
4. Betsy Z. Russell, "Idaho Panel Approves Pre-Abortion Bill," *Spokesman Review*, March 15, 2012, 1A.
5. Keogh quoted in Betsy Z. Russell, "Senate OKs Ultrasound Bill," *Spokesman Review*, March 20, 2012, 1A.
6. Russell, "Senate OKs Ultrasound Bill," 1A.
7. Bolz quoted in Betsy Z. Russell, "Idaho's Forced Ultrasound Bill May Be Dead," *Spokesman Review*, March 21, 2012, 1A.
8. Steven Ertelt, "Abortion Backers Kill Ultrasound-Abortion Bill in Idaho," *LifeNews.com*, March 27, 2012, http://www.lifenews.com/2012/03/27/abortion -backers-kill-ultrasound-abortion-bill-in-idaho/2012.
9. Dan Popkey, "Which Otter Will Decide Fate of Ultrasound Bill? Idaho's Champion of Individual Liberty Is Likely to Face a Choice between Competing Values," *Idaho Statesman* (Boise), March 20, 2012.
10. As noted later in the more thorough discussion of Elazar's typology, much of his explanation of political subculture is derived from his books *American Federalism* and *Cities of the Prairie*.
11. See Stapilus, *Paradox Politics*.
12. See Rogers, *Impact of Policy Analysis*, for a more extensive discussion of the value of case studies.
13. See Blank, *Regional Diversity of Political Values*, for a more historical description of political and social forces at work in the state.
14. For an examination of analogous changes in the country as a whole and the Republican Party at the national level see Rick Perlstein's trilogy, especially the initial volume, *Before the Storm*.

1. PETIT-IDEOLOGY

1. The description of Elazar's theory of political subcultures in the American states is derived from his two most pertinent books on the subject: *American Federalism* and *Cities of the Prairie*. This description uses aspects of both books but especially chapter 4 of *American Federalism* and chapter 6 of *Cities of the Prairie*.

2. Elazar, *American Federalism*, 110.

3. Elazar, *American Federalism*, 97.

4. Weatherby and Stapilus, *Governing Idaho*, 6.

5. Blank, *Regional Diversity of Political Values*; Devine, *Political Culture of the United States*.

6. Blank explores the origins of individualistic values in Idaho in his book *Individualism in Idaho*.

7. Blank, *Regional Diversity of Political Values*, 171–73. For additional support for the theory of cohesion among the western states concerning culture and its effect on policy see Thomas, *Politics and Public Policy in the Contemporary American West*.

8. Alm et al., "Intrastate Regional Differences in Political Culture," 117–18.

9. Stapilus, *Paradox Politics*.

10. Weatherby and Stapilus, *Governing Idaho*, 15–25.

11. For a more thorough evaluation of ideology see Eagleton, *Ideology*; and McLellan, *Ideology*.

12. Downs, *Economic Theory of Democracy*.

13. Peirce, *Mountain States of America*, 120–22.

14. Fincher et al., "Pathogen Prevalence."

15. See Burns, *Presidential Government*, for an example. In addition to the labels "Jeffersonian" and "Hamiltonian" Burns creates a "Madisonian" model, though he uses these terms quite differently from the way the terms are used here.

16. See Lind, *Land of Promise*, which uses Hamilton and Jefferson as opposite poles to describe the economic progress of the country.

17. There are almost too many books on Jefferson for any one person to read, though Ellis, *American Sphinx*, and Meacham, *Thomas Jefferson*, seem representative and better than most.

18. Ferling, *Jefferson and Hamilton*, 217.

19. As with Jefferson, there are many quality books on Hamilton. While Chernow's *Alexander Hamilton* is the gold standard, Brookhiser's *Alexander Hamilton* should not be overlooked.

20. Ferling, *Jefferson and Hamilton*, 216.

21. Lieske, "Regional Subcultures of the United States."

22. Achen and Bartels, *Democracy for Realists*.

2. PETIT-IDEOLOGY IN IDAHO

1. Glen Taylor's *The Way It Was with Me* is one of the most unusual yet entertaining memoirs by any politician.

2. For Smylie's own words about his life see his memoir, *Governor Smylie Remembers*. Much of the history that follows is taken from Governor Smylie's memoirs.

3. Smylie, *Governor Smylie Remembers*, 64.

4. Smylie, *Governor Smylie Remembers*, 64.

5. Gov. C. Ben Ross convinced the state legislature to pass a state sales tax in 1935, though it was subsequently repealed in a statewide referendum in 1936.

6. Smylie, *Governor Smylie Remembers*, 210–12.

7. Stapilus, *Paradox Politics*, 121.

8. For a firsthand account of the life of Don Samuelson see his memoir, *His Hand on My Shoulder*. Again, most of the following history is taken from Governor Samuelson's memoir.

9. Stapilus, *Paradox Politics*, 127–37. Despite Samuelson's victory, the sales tax referendum passed in a landslide. The Hamiltonian support of public schools triumphed in a confusing conclusion.

10. Stapilus, *Paradox Politics*, 140–44.

11. One of the few extensive biographies on Wilson is Smith, *James Wilson*. Much of this history of Wilson comes from Smith's biography.

12. See, for example, Hall, *Political and Legal Philosophy of James Wilson*, 21.

13. Smith, *James Wilson*, 63.

14. Smith, *James Wilson*, 89.

15. The subtitle to Carlson, *Cecil Andrus*, is *Idaho's Greatest Governor*.

16. To explore Andrus's career in his own words via the assistance of a professional writer see Andrus and Connelly, *Cecil Andrus*. That is also where you can find Andrus's definition of hornswoggling, in his introduction, titled "Hornswoggling Along."

17. Andrus and Connelly, *Cecil Andrus*, 9–11.

18. Andrus and Connelly, *Cecil Andrus*, 15.

19. See the chapter titled "Lessons from a Self-Taught Conservationist" in Andrus and Connelly, *Cecil Andrus*.

20. For a picture see Andrus and Connelly, *Cecil Andrus*, 190.

21. Andrus and Connelly, *Cecil Andrus*, 141–42.

22. Although Church wrote no memoir, three books about him stand out. Ashby and Gramer, *Fighting the Odds*, is extensive and thorough, but *Father and Son*, by his son, F. Forrester Church, and *A Lifelong Affair*, by his wife, Bethine, provide many interesting insights. Much of this history is an amalgamation of incidents taken from all of these books.

23. For a specific look at this incident see Caro, *Master of the Senate*, the third book in Caro's series on Lyndon Johnson, which includes information based on interviews with Bethine Church.

24. Steve Symms has not written a memoir, and no biography is available from other sources. Besides books on Idaho politics in general, source material includes a collection of Symms's legislative papers in the archives of the College of Idaho, located in Caldwell.

25. Stapilus, *Paradox Politics*, 190–93.

26. For a thorough biography of Jim McClure see Smallwood, *McClure of Idaho*.

27. For a thorough yet concise review of the 1980 campaign see Stapilus, *Paradox Politics*, chap. 10, "Showdown in 1980.

28. Phil Batt's memoir, *The Compleat Phil Batt*, is as unique as the man. The self-published volume includes songs, eulogies, and letters from constituents. Only a limited portion of the book is biographical in the traditional sense. His later book, *Life as a Geezer*, also provides an enlightening view of the former governor.

29. Batt, *Compleat Phil Batt*, 46–47.

30. Batt, *Compleat Phil Batt*, 39–45.

31. Stapilus, *Paradox Politics*, 194–95.

32. Stapilus, *Paradox Politics*, 194.

3. THE IDAHO STATE CONSTITUTION

1. For a thorough history of the drafting of the Idaho state constitution see Colson, *Idaho's Constitution*.

2. For a very detailed examination of every section of the Idaho state constitution see Crowley and Heffron, *Idaho State Constitution*.

3. Weatherby and Stapilus, *Governing Idaho*, 91.

4. John Miller, "Attorney General Says Idaho Vote to Privatize Liquor Might Be Illegal," *Lewiston Morning Tribune*, February 22, 2012, D4.

4. STATE LEGISLATURE

1. Cato quoted in Storing, *Complete Anti-Federalist*, 119.

2. Gary Moncrief and James B. Weatherby, "Idaho Should Reconsider Term Limits' Effect on State and Local Offices," *Idaho Statesman* (Boise), June 23, 1995, B1.

3. Squire, "Measuring State Legislative Professionalism."

4. Crotty and Jacobson, *American Parties in Decline*, 245.

5. Denney quoted in Betsy Z. Russell, "Denney Pulls Committee Chairmanships from Trail, Smith," *Eye on Boise* (blog), April 7, 2011, http://www.spokesman.com /blogs/boise/2011/apr/07/denney-pulls-committee-chairmanships-trail-smith/.

6. Dan Popkey, "Idaho House Republicans Oust Speaker Denney in a Rare Coup for a Tradition-Bound Body," *Idaho Statesman*, December 6, 2012.

7. Weatherby and Stapilus, *Governing Idaho*, 102.
8. It is not clear whether *Federalist Paper* No. 62 was written by Hamilton or Madison, so their published pseudonym, Publius, is used here.
9. Idaho Freedom Foundation, "2015 Idaho Freedom Index."
10. See Baker, *House and Senate*, for a thorough discussion of the differences between the U.S. House and Senate, especially differences due to their larger and smaller size, respectively.
11. For more details on these interviews with Idaho's legislators see LiCalzi, "Assessing Interest Group Strength on the State Level."
12. Norris quoted in Wunnicke, "Fifty Years without a Conference Committee," 21.
13. Wunnicke, "Fifty Years without a Conference Committee."
14. For an extensive review of Norris's views on the unicameral legislature see Berens, *One House*, esp. chap. 1, which is subtitled "What George Norris Said a Unicameral Would Do."
15. Weatherby and Stapilus, *Governing Idaho*, 91–92.

5. IDAHO'S GOVERNOR

1. Burns, *Presidential Government*, 29.
2. Schlesinger, "Politics of the Executive," 229; Beyle, "Governors," 202; Bowman and Kearney, *State and Local Government*, 163.
3. Bowman and Kearney, *State and Local Government*, 155.
4. Rosenthal, *Governors and Legislators*, 14.
5. It seems this has only happened three times. For details see Weatherby and Stapilus, *Governing Idaho*, 137.
6. Bachrach and Baratz, "Two Faces of Power," 952.
7. "Gov. Otter Endorses State-Run Idaho Health Exchange," *Idaho Statesman* (Boise), December 11, 2012.
8. Otter, "State of the State and Budget Address."
9. Beyle, "Governors," 456–57.
10. Weatherby and Stapilus, *Governing Idaho*, 134.
11. Batt, *Compleat Phil Batt*, 63–64.
12. Crowley and Heffron, *Idaho State Constitution*, 104–5.
13. Youtz, "Legislature Readies for Special Session," 1.
14. John Corlett, "Idaho Legislature Changes Its Makeup with Members to Be Elected by Districts," *Idaho Statesman*, March 26, 1965, 1A.
15. Robert Geddes, "Why Did Legislature Make Property Tax Changes? Commentary," *Idaho State Journal*, September 10, 2006, 21.
16. Alan Rosenthal makes a similar argument in *Governors and Legislatures*.
17. Neustadt, *Presidential Power and the Modern Presidents*, 30–31.
18. Neustadt, *Presidential Power and the Modern Presidents*, 32.

19. Smylie, *Governor Smylie Remembers*, 89–92.

20. Andrus and Connelly, *Cecil Andrus*, 190–202.

21. Andrus and Connelly, *Cecil Andrus*, 204–6.

22. Batt, *Compleat Phil Batt*, 39–45.

23. Morris, *Rise of Theodore Roosevelt*, 220.

24. "Even More Legal Drama: *Idaho v. Idaho*," *Idaho Statesman*, March 26, 2010.

25. Kristin Rodine, "In Idaho Education Reform Talks, Time and Money Are at Issue," *Idaho Statesman*, December 18, 2012.

26. Smylie, *Governor Smylie Remembers*, 173–75.

27. Stapilus, *Paradox Politics*, 200.

6. THE STATE JUDICIARY

Chapter subtitle comes from the subtitle of Sen. Joseph Clark's book *Congress: The Sapless Branch.*

1. For a more detailed though dated description of the Idaho court system see Schlechte, "State Judiciary."

2. For a decade-by-decade examination of the Idaho court system see Bianchi, *Justice for the Times.*

3. Hagan and Bianchi, "1970s: Reorganization, Growth, and Management," 176–77.

4. Miller, "1960's: The Flowering of Court Reform in Idaho," 167.

5. For details about the struggle to create the intermediate appellate court for Idaho see "The 1980's: Common Thread," in Bianchi, *Justice for the Times.*

6. Vanderpool, "Race for Justice," 1.

7. Weatherby and Stapilus in *Governing Idaho* claim justices were elected on a nonpartisan basis from 1914 to 1918 before elections again became partisan contests. Schlechte notes in "State Judiciary" (as does McFadden, "Middle Third of the Century") that nonpartisan elections began in 1934. They make no mention of any prior period of nonpartisan contests.

8. Weatherby and Stapilus, *Governing Idaho*, 123.

9. Lopeman, *Activist Advocate*, 88.

10. Vanderpool, "Race for Justice," 60.

7. LOCAL GOVERNMENT

1. Mark Barnes, "Election Guide: May 2015—Recreation District," *Kuna Melba News*, May 13, 2015.

2. Asimov, *Annotated Gulliver's Travels.*

3. Idaho State Tax Commission, "2013 Annual Report."

4. Legislative Services Office, *Special Districts in Idaho.*

5. Barnes, "Election Guide: May 2015—Recreation District."

6. Legislative Services Office, *Special Districts in Idaho*, 12.

7. Idaho Center for Fiscal Policy, *Idaho Public School Funding—1980 to 2013*, 10.

8. Ysursa, *Idaho Blue Book*, 257.

9. Ysursa, *Idaho Blue Book*, 257.

10. For an excellent description of a classic urban machine in the latter portion of the twentieth century see Royko, BOSS. For a more scholarly take see Marjorie Hershey's update (16th ed.) of *Party Politics in America*, originally compiled by Frank Sorauf and Paul Beck.

11. Of course the most vivid and self-righteous description of the urban machine is in Riordon, *Plunkitt of Tammany Hall*, with its discussion of the tenuous difference between honest graft and dishonest graft.

12. Riordon, *Plunkitt of Tammany Hall*, 11–16.

13. Sven Berg, "Strange Bedfellows: Uber and the Idaho GOP," *Idaho Statesman* (Boise), March 24, 2015.

14. Jordan quoted in Berg, "Strange Bedfellows."

8. INTEREST GROUPS IN IDAHO

1. Thomas and Hrebenar, "Interest Groups in the States," 117.

2. Nownes, "Sources of Information on Interest Groups in the American Political System," 34.

3. See Zeigler, "Effects of Lobbying," for a broader study using interviews to determine reputation.

4. Thomas and Hrebenar, "Interest Groups in the States," 118.

5. Evans, "PAC Contributions and Roll-Call Voting," 127.

6. Weatherby and Stapilus, *Governing Idaho*, 77.

7. Weatherby and Nichols, "Interest Groups in Idaho Politics."

8. Moncrief, "Idaho"; Morehouse, *State Politics, Parties and Policy*, 110.

9. Peirce, *Mountain States of America*, 136–37.

10. Thomas and Hrebenar, "Interest Groups in the States."

11. The 1977–78 and 1981–82 cycles included elections for statewide offices and the entire state legislature, while the 1979–80 cycle included only elections for the state legislature.

12. Moncrief, "Idaho," 72.

13. Weatherby and Stapilus, *Governing Idaho*, 69.

14. Moncrief, "Idaho," 71.

15. Lowery and Gray, "Dominance of Institutions in Interest Representation," 87.

16. Thomas and Hrebenar, "Interest Groups in the States."

17. Gorges, "Conducting Research on Interest Groups," 397.

18. The State of Idaho uses the term "political committee" for any group whose goal is to support or oppose a candidate or measure or that receives and spends more than $500 on a candidate or ballot measure in a calendar year. See Denney, *Sunshine Law for Political Funds and Lobbyist Activity Disclosure*, 4–5.

19. The electoral, and later operational/lobbyist, information was obtained from the website of the Office of the Secretary of State of Idaho, http://www.sos.idaho .gov/. Some data in a form more conducive for calculations and sorting were obtained directly from the Office of the Secretary of State.

20. Ysursa, "Lobbyist Registration Requirements."

21. Details on results of surveys and other data are not provided here but appear in earlier conference papers by the author or upon request. See LiCalzi, "Assessing Interest Group Strength on the State Level."

22. See Moncrief, "Idaho," for spending in the 1970s and 1980s.

23. Moncrief, "Idaho," 71.

24. Moncrief, "Idaho," 71.

25. Again, for more details of the interviews see LiCalzi, "Assessing Interest Group Strength on the State Level."

9. POLITICAL PARTIES

1. Although detailed histories of political parties in Idaho in the nineteenth century are slim, Stapilus, *Paradox Politics*, provides an interesting history of Idaho politics in the twentieth century in a very readable narrative form. Much of the following is based on that source.

2. See Malone, *C. Ben Ross and the New Deal in Idaho*, for a complete study of Ross and Idaho.

3. Taylor's autobiography, *The Way It Was with Me*, is a must-read for anyone interested in Idaho politics. It is like no other political biography anywhere.

4. Stapilus and Peterson, *Idaho 100*, 10.

5. Stapilus and Peterson, *Idaho 100*, 99–101.

6. Batt, *Compleat Phil Batt*, 29.

7. Parker and Davidson, "Why Do Americans Love Their Congressmen So Much More Than Their Congress?"

8. Andrus and Connelly, *Cecil Andrus*, 11.

9. Paul Krugman provides a detailed though one-sided description of this change in his book *Conscience of a Liberal*.

10. Perlstein, *Nixonland*; Perlstein, *Invisible Bridge*.

11. Frank, *What's the Matter with Kansas?*

10. INTERGOVERNMENTAL RELATIONS

1. The term "national" is used throughout this book instead of the more colloquial "federal" since the entire system is federal.

2. One of the best appraisals of American federalism in all of its facets is Robertson, *Federalism and the Making of America*.

3. Clinton v. Cedar Rapids and the Missouri River Railroad (24 Iowa 455; 1868).

4. This phrase originates in Neustadt, *Presidential Power*.

5. For the definitive explanation of the law and its origins, Miles's own article, "Origin and Meaning of Miles' Law," is the obvious source.

6. Probably the best explanation of institutional rational choice theory comes from Kiser and Ostrom, "Three Worlds of Action."

7. Lewin, *Principles of Topological Psychology*.

8. Read, *Power versus Liberty*, 85.

9. Ferling, *Jefferson and Hamilton*, 217–18.

10. Hamilton quoted in Ferling, *Jefferson and Hamilton*, 119–20.

11. Hamilton quoted in Read, *Power versus Liberty*, 72.

12. Read, *Power versus Liberty*, 72.

13. Ferling, *Jefferson and Hamilton*, 216.

14. Ferling, *Jefferson and Hamilton*, 145.

15. Hamilton, Madison, and Jay, *Federalist Papers*, No. 70, 354.

16. For a thorough yet reasonably comprehensible exploration of public choice theory see Mueller, *Public Choice*.

17. Read, *Power versus Liberty*, 128–33.

18. Ferling, *Jefferson and Hamilton*, 304–5.

19. Ferling, *Jefferson and Hamilton*, 195.

20. Stapilus, *Paradox Politics*, 194.

21. John Miller, "Vote against Patriot Act Still Defines Butch Otter," *Lewiston Morning Tribune*, September 5, 2011, C3.

22. Betsy Z. Russell, "Otter's Hard Line Softens over Time: Pragmatism Grows Since '70s Elections," *Spokesman Review* (Spokane WA), May 17, 2009, 1A.

23. Stapilus quoted in Russell, "Otter's Hard Line Softens over Time," 1A.

EPILOGUE

1. Harrison Berry and George Prentice, "UPDATE: War of Words Ignites among Idaho GOP in Wake of Defeat of Child Support Measure," *Boise Weekly*, April 12, 2015.

2. Betsy Z. Russell, "Idaho Passes Child Support Enforcement Bill, though Most North Idaho Lawmakers Vote No," *Spokesman Review* (Spokane WA), May 18, 2015.

3. Betsy Z. Russell "Otter Signs Child Support Bill, State Leaders Say Claims It's Unconstitutional Are 'Bogus,'" *Spokesman Review*, May 19, 2015.

4. Malek quoted in Berry and Prentice, "UPDATE: War of Words Ignites among Idaho GOP."

5. Malek quoted in Berry and Prentice, "UPDATE: War of Words Ignites among Idaho GOP."

6. Luke Malek, "Rep. Luke Malek: Idaho Should Resist Politics of Obedience," *Spokesman Review*, May 17, 2015; Wayne Hoffman, "Ambitious Malek the Poster Boy for Obedience to Federal Government," Idaho Freedom Foundation, May 18, 2015, http://idahofreedom.org/ambitious-malek-the-poster-boy-of-obedience -to-federal-government/.

7. See Kahneman, *Thinking, Fast and Slow*; and Thaler, *Misbehaving*, for more detail on this concept of decision-making.

Achen, Christopher H., and Larry M. Bartels. *Democracy for Realists: Why Elections Do Not Produce Responsive Government*. Princeton NJ: Princeton University Press, 2016.

Alm, Leslie R., Ross E. Burkhart, W. David Patton, and James B. Weatherby. "Intrastate Regional Differences in Political Culture: A Case Study of Idaho." *State and Local Government Review* 33, no. 2 (2001): 109–19.

Andrus, Cecil, and Joel Connelly. *Cecil Andrus: Politics Western Style*. Seattle: Sasquatch, 1998.

Ashby, LeRoy, and Rod Gramer. *Fighting the Odds: The Life of Senator Frank Church*. Pullman: Washington State University Press, 1994.

Asimov, Isaac, ed. *The Annotated "Gulliver's Travels,"* by Jonathan Swift. New York: Potter, 1980.

Bachrach, Peter, and Morton S. Baratz. "Two Faces of Power." *American Political Science Review* 56, no. 4 (1962): 947–52.

Baker, Ross K. *House and Senate*. 4th ed. New York: Norton, 2008.

Batt, Phil. *The Compleat Phil Batt: A Kaleidoscope*. Self-published, n.d.

——— . *Life as a Geezer*. Self-published, n.d.

Berens, Charlyne. *One House: The Unicameral's Progressive Vision for Nebraska*. Lincoln: University of Nebraska Press, 2005.

Beyle, Thad. "Governors." In *Politics in the American States: A Comparative Analysis*, edited by Virginia Gray, Herbert Jacob, and Kenneth N. Vines, 180–221. 4th ed. Boston: Little, Brown, 1983.

Bianchi, Carl F., ed. *Justice for the Times: A Centennial History of the Idaho State Courts*. Boise: Idaho Law Foundation, 1990.

Blank, Robert H. *Individualism in Idaho: The Territorial Foundations*. Pullman: Washington State University Press, 1988.

——— . *Regional Diversity of Political Values: Idaho Political Culture*. Washington DC: University Press of America, 1978.

Bowman, Ann O'M., and Richard C. Kearney. *State and Local Government: The Essentials*. 2nd ed. Boston: Houghton Mifflin, 2003.

Brookhiser, Richard. *Alexander Hamilton: American*. New York: Free Press, 1999.

Burns, James MacGregor. *Presidential Government: The Crucible for Leadership*. Boston: Houghton Mifflin, 1965.

Carlson, Chris. *Cecil Andrus: Idaho's Greatest Governor*. Caldwell ID: Caxton, 2011.

Caro, Robert A. *The Years of Lyndon Johnson: Master of the Senate*. New York: Knopf, 2002.

Chernow, Ron. *Alexander Hamilton*. New York: Penguin Books, 2004.

Church, Bethine. *A Lifelong Affair: My Passion for People and Politics*. Washington DC: Francis Press, 2003.

Church, F. Forrester. *Father and Son: A Personal Biography of Senator Frank Church of Idaho*. New York: Harper and Row, 1985.

Clark, Joseph S. *Congress: The Sapless Branch*. New York: Harper and Row, 1964.

Cohler, Anne M., Basia C. Miller, and Harold S. Stone, eds. *Montesquieu: The Spirit of the Laws*. Translated by the editors. New York: Cambridge University Press, 1989.

Colson, Dennis. *Idaho's Constitution: The Tie That Binds*. Moscow: University of Idaho Press, 1991.

Cronin, Thomas E., and Robert D. Loevy. *Colorado Politics and Policy: Governing a Purple State*. Lincoln: University of Nebraska Press, 2012.

Crotty, William J., and Gary C. Jacobson. *American Parties in Decline*. Boston: Little, Brown, 1980.

Crowley, Donald, and Florence Heffron. *The Idaho State Constitution: A Reference Guide*. Westport CT: Greenwood, 1994.

Denney, Lawerence, Idaho Secretary of State. *The Sunshine Law for Political Funds and Lobbyist Activity Disclosure*. Boise ID: Office of the Secretary of State, 2015.

Devine, Donald J. *The Political Culture of the United States*. Boston: Little, Brown, 1972.

Downs, Anthony. *An Economic Theory of Democracy*. New York: Harper, 1957.

Eagleton, Terry. *Ideology: An Introduction*. London: Verso, 1991.

Elazar, Daniel J. *American Federalism: A View from the States*. New York: Thomas Crowell, 1966.

———. *Cities of the Prairie: The Metropolitan Frontier and American Politics*. New York: Basic Books, 1970.

Ellis, Joseph J. *American Sphinx: The Character of Thomas Jefferson*. New York: Vintage Books, 1998.

Evans, Diana M. "PAC Contributions and Roll-Call Voting." In *Interest Group Politics*, edited by Allan J. Cigler and Burdett A. Loomis. Washington DC: CQ Press, 1986.

Ferling, John. *Jefferson and Hamilton: The Rivalry That Forged a Nation*. New York: Bloomsbury, 2013.

Fincher, Corey L., Randy Thornhill, Damian R. Murray, and Mark Schaller. "Pathogen Prevalence Predicts Human Cross-Cultural Variability in Individualism/Collectivism." *Proceedings: Biological Sciences* 275, no. 1640 (2008): 1279–85.

Frank, Thomas. *What's the Matter with Kansas? How Conservatives Won the Heart of America.* New York: Henry Holt, 2004.

Gorges, Michael J. "Conducting Research on Interest Groups." In *Research Guide to U.S. and International Interest Groups,* edited by Clive S. Thomas. Westport CT: Praeger, 2004.

Hagan, Alfred C., and Carl F. Bianchi. "The 1970s: Reorganization, Growth, and Management." In *Justice for the Times: A Centennial History of the Idaho State Courts,* edited by Carl F. Bianchi. Boise: Idaho Law Foundation, 1990.

Hall, Mark David. *The Political and Legal Philosophy of James Wilson, 1742–1798.* Columbia: University of Missouri Press, 1997.

Hamilton, Alexander, James Madison, and John Jay. *The Federalist Papers.* Edited by Ian Shapiro. New Haven CT: Yale University Press, 2009.

Hershey, Marjorie Randon. *Party Politics in America.* 16th ed. New York: Routledge, 2016.

Hetherington, Marc J., and Thomas J. Rudolph. *Why Washington Won't Work.* Chicago: University of Chicago Press, 2015.

Hirschman, Albert O. *Exit, Voice, and Loyalty: Responses to Decline in Firms, Organizations, and States.* Cambridge MA: Harvard University Press, 1970.

Hoffman, Wayne. "Ambitious Malek the Poster Boy for Obedience to Federal Government." Idaho Freedom Foundation, May 18, 2015. http://idahofreedom.org /ambitious-malek-the-poster-boy-of-obedience-to-federal-government/.

Hrebenar, Ronald, and Clive S. Thomas, eds. *Interest Group Politics in the American West.* Salt Lake City: University of Utah Press, 1987.

Idaho Center for Fiscal Policy. *Idaho Public School Funding—1980 to 2013.* Boise: ICFP, 2014.

Idaho Freedom Foundation. "2015 Idaho Freedom Index." March 21, 2015. http:// idahofreedomindex.com/.

Idaho State Tax Commission. "2013 Annual Report." March 21, 2015. http://tax.idaho .gov/reports/EPB00033_12-20-2013.pdf.

Kahneman, Daniel. *Thinking, Fast and Slow.* New York: Farrar, Straus, and Giroux, 2011.

Kincaid, John, ed. *Political Culture, Public Policy and the American States.* Philadelphia: Institute for the Study of Human Issues, 1982.

Kiser, Larry L., and Elinor Ostrom. "The Three Worlds of Action: A Metatheoretical Synthesis of Institutional Approaches." In *Strategies of Political Inquiry,* edited by Elinor Ostrom. Beverly Hills CA: SAGE, 1982.

Krugman, Paul. *The Conscience of a Liberal.* New York: Norton, 2007.

Legislative Services Office, State of Idaho. *Special Districts in Idaho.* Boise ID: LSO, 2014.

Legislature of the State of Idaho. Senate. State Affairs Committee. Senate Bill No. 1387. 61st Legislature, 2nd regular session, 2012.

Lewin, Kurt. *Principles of Topological Psychology.* New York: McGraw-Hill, 1936.

LiCalzi, Jasper. "Assessing Interest Group Strength on the State Level." Paper presented at the annual meeting of the Western Political Science Association, Vancouver BC, March 18–19, 2009.

Lieske, Joel. "Regional Subcultures of the United States." *Journal of Politics* 55, no. 4 (1993): 888–913.

Lind, Michael. *Land of Promise: An Economic History of the United States.* New York: Harper, 2012.

Lopeman, Charles C. *The Activist Advocate: Policy Making in State Supreme Courts.* Westport CT: Praeger, 1999.

Lowery, David, and Virginia Gray. "The Dominance of Institutions in Interest Representation: A Test of Seven Explanations." *American Journal of Political Science* 42 (January 1998): 231–55.

Malone, Michael P. *C. Ben Ross and the New Deal in Idaho.* Seattle: University of Washington Press, 1970.

Martin, Boyd A. "IDAHO: The Sectional State." In *Politics in the American West*, edited by Frank H. Jonas. Salt Lake City: University of Utah Press, 1969.

McFadden, Joseph J. 1990. "The Middle Third of the Century: The War Years and the Depression." In *Justice for the Times: A Centennial History of the Idaho State Courts*, edited by Carl F. Bianchi. Boise: Idaho Law Foundation, 1990.

McLellan, David. *Ideology.* Minneapolis: University of Minnesota Press, 1986.

Meacham, Jon. *Thomas Jefferson: The Art of Power.* New York: Random House, 2012.

Miles, Rufus E., Jr. "The Origin and Meaning of Miles' Law." *Public Administration Review* 38, no. 5 (1978): 399–403.

Miller, Thomas. 1990. "The 1960's: The Flowering of Court Reform in Idaho." In *Justice for the Times: A Centennial History of the Idaho State Courts*, edited by Carl F. Bianchi. Boise: Idaho Law Foundation, 1990.

Moncrief, Gary. "Idaho: The Interests of Sectionalism." In *Interest Group Politics in the American West*, edited by Ronald J. Hrebenar and Clive S. Thomas. Salt Lake City: University of Utah Press, 1987.

Morehouse, Sarah McCally. *State Politics, Parties and Policy.* New York: Holt, Rinehart, and Winston, 1981.

Morris, Edmund. *The Rise of Theodore Roosevelt.* New York: Modern Library, 1979.

Mueller, Dennis C. *Public Choice.* Cambridge: Cambridge University Press, 1979.

Neustadt, Richard E. *Presidential Power and the Modern Presidents: The Politics of Leadership from Roosevelt to Reagan.* New York: Free Press, 1990.

Nichols, Glenn W., Ray C. Jolly, and Boyd A. Martin, eds. *State and Local Government in Idaho: A Reader.* Moscow: Bureau of Public Affairs Research, University of Idaho, 1970.

Norman, Jesse. *Edmund Burke: The First Conservative.* New York: Basic Books, 2013.

Nownes, Anthony J. "Sources of Information on Interest Groups in the American Political System: An Overview." In *Research Guide to U.S. and International Interest Groups*, edited by Clive S. Thomas. Westport CT: Praeger, 2004.

Otter, C. L. "Butch." "State of the State and Budget Address." January 7, 2013. http://gov .idaho.gov/mediacenter/speeches/sp_2013/State%20of%20the%20state%202013.pdf.

Parker, Glenn R., and Roger H. Davidson. "Why Do Americans Love Their Congressmen So Much More Than Their Congress?" *Legislative Studies Quarterly* 4, no. 1 (1979): 53–61.

Peirce, Neal R. *The Mountain States of America: People, Politics, and Power in the Eight Rocky Mountain States*. New York: Norton, 1972.

Perlstein, Rick. *Before the Storm: Barry Goldwater and the Unmaking of the American Consensus*. New York: Hill and Wang, 2001.

———. *The Invisible Bridge: The Fall of Nixon and the Rise of Reagan*. New York: Simon and Schuster, 2014.

———. *Nixonland: The Rise of a President and the Fracturing of America*. New York: Scribner, 2008.

Read, James H. *Power versus Liberty: Madison, Hamilton, Wilson, and Jefferson*. Charlottesville: University Press of Virginia, 2000.

Riker, William H. *Liberalism against Populism: A Confrontation between the Theory of Democracy and the Theory of Social Choice*. Long Grove IL: Waveland, 1982.

Riordon, William L. *Plunkitt of Tammany Hall*. New York: Dutton, 1963.

Roberts, Alasdair. *America's First Great Depression: Economic Crisis and Political Disorder after the Panic of 1837*. Ithaca NY: Cornell University Press, 2012.

Robertson, David Brian. *Federalism and the Making of America*. New York: Routledge, 2012.

Rogers, James M. *The Impact of Policy Analysis*. Pittsburgh: University of Pittsburgh Press, 1988.

Rosenthal, Alan. *Governors and Legislators: Contending Powers*. Washington DC: Congressional Quarterly, 1990.

Royko, Mike. BOSS: *Richard J. Daley of Chicago*. New York: Plume, 1971.

Samuelson, Don W. *His Hand on My Shoulder: A Life Story of Hunting, Fishing, Love and Politics*. Sandpoint ID: Parbest and Dickeons, 1993.

Schlechte, Myran. "The State Judiciary." In *State and Local Government in Idaho: A Reader*, edited by Glenn W. Nichols, Ray C. Jolly, and Boyd A. Martin. Moscow: Bureau of Public Affairs Research, University of Idaho, 1970.

Schlesinger, Joseph A. "The Politics of the Executive." In *Politics in the American States: A Comparative Analysis*, edited by Virginia Gray, Herbert Jacob, and Kenneth N. Vines, 207–37. Boston: Little, Brown, 1965.

Smallwood, William L. *McClure of Idaho*. Caldwell ID: Caxton, 2007.

Smith, Charles Page. *James Wilson: Founding Father, 1742–1798*. Chapel Hill: University of North Carolina Press, 1956.

Smylie, Robert E. *Governor Smylie Remembers*. Moscow: University of Idaho Press, 1998.

Squire, Peverill. "Measuring State Legislative Professionalism." In *The Lanahan Readings in State and Local Government: Diversity, Innovation, Rejuvenation*, edited by John R. Baker. 2nd ed. Baltimore MD: Lanahan, 2010.

Stapilus, Randy. *It Happened in Idaho*. Guilford CT: Globe Pequot, 2002.

——. *Paradox Politics: People and Power in Idaho*. Boise ID: Ridenbaugh, 1988.

Stapilus, Randy, and Martin Peterson. *Idaho 100: The People Who Most Influenced the Gem State*. Carlton OR: Ridenbaugh, 2012.

Storing, Herbert J. *The Complete Anti-Federalist*. Vol. 1. Chicago: University of Chicago Press, 1981.

Taylor, Glen H. *The Way It Was with Me*. Secaucus NJ: Lyle Stuart, 1970.

Thaler, Richard H. *Misbehaving: The Making of Behavioral Economics*. New York: Norton, 2015.

Thomas, Clive, ed. *Politics and Public Policy in the Contemporary American West*. Albuquerque: University of New Mexico Press, 1991.

Thomas, Clive S., and Ronald L. Hrebenar. "Interest Groups in the States." In *Politics in the American States*, edited by Virginia Gray and Russell L. Hanson. 8th ed. Washington DC: CQ Press, 2004.

Vanderpool, Rachel T. "The Race for Justice: Analysis of Citizens Survey of Idaho's Judicial Election Process." Twin Falls ID: Institute for Court Management, 2003.

Weatherby, James B., and Glenn W. Nichols. "Interest Groups in Idaho Politics." In *State and Local Government in Idaho: A Reader*, edited by Glenn W. Nichols, Ray C. Jolly, and Boyd A. Martin. Moscow: Bureau of Public Affairs Research, University of Idaho, 1970.

Weatherby, James B., and Randy Stapilus. *Governing Idaho: Politics, People and Power*. Caldwell ID: Caxton, 2005.

Wunnicke, Pat. "Fifty Years without a Conference Committee." *State Legislatures* 13, no. 9 (1987): 20–23.

Youtz, Jeff. "Legislature Readies for Special Session." *Legislative Perspective* (Idaho Legislative Services Office) 14, no. 3 (2006).

Ysursa, Ben, Idaho Secretary of State. *Idaho Blue Book: 2013–2014*. Boise ID: Caxton, 2014.

——. "Lobbyist Registration Requirements." Elections, Campaign Disclosure and Lobbyists, Idaho Secretary of State, 2015. http://www.sos.idaho.gov/elect/lobbyist/lobbyist.htm.

Zeigler, Harmon. "The Effects of Lobbying: A Comparative Assessment." In *Comparative Legislative Systems: A Reader in Theory and Research*, edited by Herbert Hirsch and M. Donald Hancock. New York: Free Press, 1971.

racial issues, 107, 108

rational choice theory, 114–15, 137n6

rationing, gasoline/rubber, 99

Reagan, Ronald, 18, 26, 27, 107, 108, 109

real estate activity, 93

reapportionment, 58, 71, 101

Redford, Robert, 103

religion, 107; freedom of, 33

Report on Manufactures (Hamilton), 117

Republican Coordinating Committee (RCC), 18

Republican in name only (RINO), 8

Republican National Committee, 18

Republican Party, xvii, 17, 20, 27, 29, 84, 108; alliance with, 99; closed primaries and, 72; dominance of, 102, 110; Idaho and, 97–98, 98–102; rise of, 109; shift in, 18; success for, 106

Republicans, xiv, 106; Democrats and, 31, 47, 70, 125; Hamiltonian, 26

responsibility, 33, 58, 61, 77, 112, 113, 126, 127

Revolutionary War, 116, 117

Reynolds v. Sims, 58

rights, 11, 32–34, 49, 65; civil, 25, 107, 113; crime victims, 33; criminal defendants, 71; curtailment of, 37; individual, 9, 41; minority, 118; political, 64; property, 5, 9, 125; water, 34; women's, 108

right- to-life, xiii

"right- to-work" law, 18, 105

Risch, Jim, 58, 62

River of No Return Wilderness, 25

Robertson, Pat, 109

Robins, C. A., 16

Rockefeller, Nelson, 17

Rocky Flats, nuclear waste from, 60

Roe v. Wade, 24, 64

Romney, Mitt, 97

Roosevelt, Franklin D., 107

Ross, C. Ben, 99, 100, 130n5

Rousseau, Jean-Jacques, 9

sales tax, 17, 18, 19, 23, 58, 131n9

Samuelson, Don, 100, 102; Andrus and, 23; election of, 18, 53; sales tax and, 19, 131n9; term of, 19–20

Sanders, Bernie, 30

San Francisco Chronicle, on Taylor, 100

Schlesinger, Joseph, 53

Second Amendment, 33

secretary of state, 61, 90

segregation, 71, 112

self-interest, 2, 3, 39, 40, 126

senators: selection process for, 45; terms for, 45–46, 48

Sharia Law, 124

Shays's Rebellion, 116

Silak, Cathy, 69

Simms, Kim, 124

slavery, 11, 21

Small Claims Department, 66

Smith, Leon: removal of, 43

Smith, Robert, 26

Smylie, Robert, 26, 53, 63, 100, 131n2; appointment by, 62; as Hamiltonian, 16–18; Idaho constitution and, 36; public schools and, 17; sales tax and, 18, 19; special session and, 58; terms for, 59

social issues, 4; Hamiltonian approach on, 107, 108, 109; Jeffersonian approach on, 107, 108

Socialist Party, 98

social science, 10, 128

society: best outcomes for, 11; culture and, 7; divisions within, xiv; goals of, 8; liberal understanding of, 10; objectives of, 6; political context of, xv, xvi

Nevada Politics and Government:
Conservatism in an Open Society
By Don W. Driggs and
Leonard E. Goodall

New Jersey Politics and
Government: Suburban Politics
Comes of Age, second edition
By Barbara G. Salmore and
Stephen A. Salmore

New York Politics and Government:
Competition and Compassion
By Sarah F. Liebschutz, with Robert W.
Bailey, Jeffrey M. Stonecash, Jane
Shapiro Zacek, and Joseph F.
Zimmerman

North Carolina Government and Politics
By Jack D. Fleer

Oklahoma Politics and Policies:
Governing the Sooner State
By David R. Morgan, Robert E.
England, and George G. Humphreys

Oregon Politics and
Government: Progressives versus
Conservative Populists
By Richard A. Clucas, Mark
Henkels, and Brent S. Steel

Rhode Island Politics and Government
By Maureen Moakley and
Elmer Cornwell

South Carolina Politics and Government
By Cole Blease Graham Jr. and
William V. Moore

Utah Politics and Government:
American Democracy among a
Unique Electorate
By Adam R. Brown

West Virginia Politics and Government
By Richard A. Brisbin Jr., Robert
Jay Dilger, Allan S. Hammock,
and Christopher Z. Mooney

West Virginia Politics and
Government, second edition
By Richard A. Brisbin Jr., Robert
Jay Dilger, Allan S. Hammock,
and L. Christopher Plein

Wisconsin Politics and Government:
America's Laboratory of Democracy
By James K. Conant

To order or obtain more information on these or other University of Nebraska Press
titles, visit nebraskapress.unl.edu.

CPSIA information can be obtained
at www.ICGtesting.com
Printed in the USA
LVHW092016171118
597514LV00006B/413/P